TAKING HER SERIOUSLY

TAKING HER SERIOUSLY

Penelope &
the Plot of Homer's
ODYSSEY

Richard Heitman

THE UNIVERSITY OF MICHIGAN PRESS
ANN ARBOR

For Heidi & Don

Copyright © by the University of Michigan 2005
All rights reserved
Published in the United States of America by
The University of Michigan Press
Manufactured in the United States of America
⊚ Printed on acid-free paper

2008   2007   2006   2005   4   3   2   1

A CIP catalog record for this book is available from the British Library.

Library of Congress Cataloging-in-Publication Data

Heitman, Richard, 1952–
     Taking her seriously : Penelope & the plot of Homer's Odyssey / Richard Heitman.
         p. cm.
     Includes bibliographical references and index.
     ISBN 0-472-11489-1 (cloth : alk. paper)
     1. Homer. Odyssey.   2. Homer—Characters—Penelope.   3. Epic poetry, Greek—History
and criticism.   4. Penelope (Greek mythology) in literature.   5. Separation (Psychology)
in literature.   6. Women and literature—Greece.   7. Married women in literature.
8. Women in literature.   I. Title.

   PA4167.H45   2005
   883.01—dc22

2005041766

Acknowledgments

This book is dedicated to Heidi Hollmann, my wife, my love, and my best critic and to the memory of my father Donald Stemler Heitman who taught me how to follow a trail by starlight. Many others have also helped make this book possible. I offer my heartfelt gratitude to the following: Paul Friedrich, the greatest of teachers and a brave heart, for his steadfast belief in me and in this project; Wendy Doniger, for asking questions that I wrestled with to the very end; David Tracy, for an uncanny ability to spark some of his own brilliance in others; Hardy Hansen, Gregory Sifakis, and Helma Dik, for reading Greek with me; Walter Hollmann, for German; James Redfield for candor and a stern professional eye; Peter Crombie, my oldest friend and longtime collaborator, for those countless hours spent on getting more than an academic knowledge of the structure of drama; Jean-Michel Robert, for patiently helping me early on to focus the idea of this book and set the right tone; the National Endowment for the Humanities, for three priceless summers; Alan Wallace for looking at the manuscript so carefully; Christopher Collins and the University of Michigan Press, for speed, decision, and commitment; John Ketterer and Steve Frank, for their truly miraculous generosity that kept the whole dream from collapsing; and Ellen Seidel, for promising to be a classicist some day.

ΟΡΟΣΟΥΧΟΡΟΣ

Contents

Introduction

The *Odyssey* opens upon a fortuitous event. Poseidon, the sole god preventing the return of the hero Odysseus to his homeland, has gone to the far-off country of the Ethiopians to savor the sacrificial feast that they have prepared in his honor. The sea god's absence affords Athene a rare opportunity to secure Odysseus's release from Ogygia, where the hero has been languishing for seven years, in and out of the arms of the nymph Calypso. Athene exhorts Zeus to dispatch Hermes immediately to the island so that "with all speed" (*Od.* 1.85) Hermes may command Calypso to release the captive. Speed is well warranted, since Poseidon's absence is temporary. In fact, because Zeus neglects to dispatch Hermes for a whole six days, Poseidon does indeed return before Odysseus has sailed to safety, and the angered god calls down a violent storm that all but drowns the hero. For her part, Athene could easily have prevented Zeus's nearly disastrous delay. She might have stayed on Olympus to keep pressure on her father or gone herself to Ogygia to secure Odysseus's release. Instead, she makes a bee-line for Ithaca, where apparently something even more important than Odysseus's freedom is at stake.

Like Athene, this book will head straight for Ithaca, where it will find Penelope, to whom Odysseus said when he departed for Troy, "Here let everything be in your charge" (*Od.* 18.266). This book, then, will attempt to take Penelope seriously, as the one responsible for the welfare of the household that Odysseus left behind and that is now so oppressed with trouble.

Many writers have taken Penelope seriously. Traditionally, Penelope has been accorded very serious status as the perfect wife, the model woman, a paragon of patience, or a saint of faithfulness. More recently, there have been a great many serious and successful attempts to renew interest in various aspects of her place in the *Odyssey*. For example, John Winkler and many others emphasize her similarity to Odysseus; Nancy Felson-Rubin and Marilyn Katz explore the complexity and indeterminacy of her character and motivations; Lydia Allione, Agathe Thornton, and Uvo Hölscher argue for her greater role in the plot; and Froma Zeitlin and Helene Foley champion Penelope's importance for the epic's philosophy and theme. John Finley recognized the importance of Penelope in his 1978 book Homer's "*Odyssey*," which he opened with a chapter on her. To Finley, the central theme of the *Odyssey* is "life brought home, therefore, finally shared," and he argues that "Penelope is the central figure of home [since] she both kept it in existence and makes it recoverable" (4). Finley cites Agamemnon's encomiastic praise of Penelope's virtue and his prediction of her great future fame.

"O fortunate son of Laertes, Odysseus of many devices,
surely you won yourself a wife endowed with great virtue.
How good was proved the heart that is in blameless Penelope,
Ikarios' daughter, and how well she remembered Odysseus,
her wedded husband. Thereby the fame of her virtue shall
    never
die away, but the immortals will make for the people
of earth a thing of grace in the song for prudent Penelope.

                       (*Od.* 24.192–98)[1]

"That," Finley says, "comes near making our *Odysseia* a *Penelopeia*" (1978, 3–4).

I doubt that the *Odyssey* needs to be renamed to justify my approach to it, though I intend to make the strongest case possible for Penelope's centrality to the plot. Indeed, the subject of this book will be the structure of the *Odyssey* as it emerges from the domestic concerns of Odysseus's family, while its major assumption will be that Penelope is the principal agent of a plot so conceived. In addition, taking her seriously also means, for me, accepting Penelope as a reliable reporter of her own mind, that is, of her own concerns, motivations, and intentions.

This sort of approach to the *Odyssey* has been neglected, for several powerful reasons, many of which underpin the dominant critical approaches to the *Odyssey* to date. First, the critics of the analytic school, in their concern to find the authentic core of the Homeric poems (that which was supposed to have come directly from the hand or mind of Homer), have tended to discount the importance of whatever smacks of post-Homeric influence. Whole sections of the *Odyssey*—for example, Telemachos's adventures in Pylos and Sparta—are excluded from their analyses. R. D. Dawe's translation and commentary is the most recent edition of the *Odyssey* influenced by the analytic approach. Dawe employs two different point sizes for the typeface of the translation, one for acceptable passages and a smaller size for passages that are "suspect" (in roman type) and for those that "have no right to be there" (in italic).[2] Penelope is often a victim of this practice; all references to her weaving and unweaving of a shroud for Laertes in order to forestall the suitors are writ small.

Almost as much effort has been made to discover flawed narrative elements as has been exerted to discover inauthentic lines. Such a critical approach focuses on the primitive folkloric tales that lie behind the epic and casts the poet in the role of an extremely talented weaver of the various strands. The material, however, is considered to have been ultimately too diverse for seamless synthesis. Book 19 is the obvious target of this criticism. In that book, Homer is supposed to have made a serious blunder by failing to assign Penelope an adequate motivation for her decision to initiate the contest of the bow. G. S. Kirk finds "a serious illogicality which supports the probability that an earlier version, in which the contest was arranged in full collusion between husband and wife, has been extensively but inadequately remodeled by the large-scale composer" (1962, 246–47). Though Finley makes the claim "Because Penelope's decision for the test of the bow makes possible Odysseus's homecoming, she is a key to the unity of the poem" (1978, 2), the persistent narratological difficulties with this passage have done a great deal to marginalize her. Penelope is thought to be forced to act completely out of character for the sake of advancing Homer's plot. W. J. Woodhouse complains:

> Willy nilly, one or other of the actors in the story must do something, in order that the whole thing may go forward. If the poet cannot find in his characters what he needs in the way of

motive power, he must just contribute it out of his own head.
(1930, 87)

The idea behind this reading is that in an attempt to salvage his plot, Homer was forced to sacrifice the integrity of Penelope's character. This approach inevitably frustrates any attempt to study Penelope as a consistent character.

Whereas the analytic school is unforgiving of inconsistencies of plot in its eagerness to marginalize everything that does not square with its notion of Homer's genius, the reaction to that school led by the theories of oral composition that Perry and Lord championed takes a contrary approach. According to these theories, apparent inconsistencies in Penelope's character pose little cause for wonder or study. Instead, like many other errors that are forgiven the oral poet, they would seem to flow naturally from the difficulties of oral composition and from the singer's continual need to vary his song, rather than from any shortcomings of interpretation.

Since the approaches I have already discussed tend to deny unity to the plot of the *Odyssey*—a unity, I believe, on which an appreciation of Penelope's character depends—I must hold them in abeyance. Even many approaches that do accept unity of plot in the *Odyssey* do little for the understanding of Penelope. For example, Aristotle, defending the plot of the *Odyssey* as similar to tragedy in that it is built around a single action, insists that the action is Odysseus's *nostos* (homecoming).

> A certain man has been away from home for many years,
> kept that way by Poseidon, and he ends up being alone.
> Meanwhile, his affairs at home are in such a state that his
> wife's suitors are squandering his property and are plotting
> against his son. Tempest-tossed, he arrives home; he
> reveals himself to some; he attacks and destroys his
> enemies and is saved. That is the essence of the *Odyssey*;
> the rest is made up of episodes.
>
> (*Poetics* 1455b17–24)

The treatment of the *Odyssey* as essentially a *nostos* story obviously discourages focus on Ithaca and Penelope, and this tradition tends to take the privileging of Odysseus to extremes. As I was writing this introduction, I came upon the abridgment that Stanley Lombardo has lately made of his fine translations of the *Iliad* and the *Odyssey*. He entitles it *The Essential Homer*. Sadly, I was not overly surprised to discover that almost all passages that did not feature Odysseus were eliminated.³ No reader restricted to this "essential" Homer would be able to recognize the complexity of the crisis in Ithaca, appreciate the seriousness of the threat to Telemachos, or guess that Penelope had any serious agency in the plot.

Marcel Detienne and Jean-Pierre Vernant—especially in their 1978 *Cunning Intelligence in Greek Culture and Society*—opened a new and productive chapter in the study of the *Odyssey*. Their concentration on *mētis* as one of the principal themes of the epic brought into sharp focus much that had been obscure. Scholarship had not previously ignored the theme; it had just never embraced it. *Mētis* could not help but strike many minds as embarrassingly less than noble. The difficulty is that *mētis*, though translated benignly as "cunning intelligence," cannot be distinguished—except quite artificially—from deception and mendacity. From classical times onward, the trickster, the deceiver, or the inveterate liar who relished his lies was a rogue. Sophocles' disdainful portrait of Odysseus in the *Philoctetes* is a typical response to this unheroic character. Fortunately, Detienne and Vernant managed to demonstrate to critics how to recognize *mētis* as a virtue. The anthropologist Michael Herzfeld—through his studies of present-day Greece and their influence on the classicist John Winkler—also helped point the way toward appreciation of the importance of secrecy and lying, which Greeks still consider "unfortunate necessities but which they nonetheless practice diligently, constantly, and craftily" (Winkler 1990, 134).

I further accept John Peradotto's insistence that *mētis* is not only a fundamental theme of the *Odyssey* but integral to Odysseus's own identity. In his insightful *Man in the Middle Voice*, Peradotto analyzes the wonderful *paranomasia* of book 9 by which Homer takes pains to link Odysseus's identity to the idea of cunning. The Greek word *mētis* (cunning) sounds like *mē tis* (nobody), which, by grammatical transformation, becomes *ou tis* (nobody). *Outis*, understood as a proper noun ("Nobody"), is the name that Odysseus gives for himself to the Cyclops. Homer takes pains to identify *outis* with *mētis*. Peradotto writes,

> We have suggested that Odysseus under the name of Outis represents the fundamental potentiality of the narrative "subject"

to take on any attribute, to be linked with any action. It is therefore associated with *mētis*, that hidden power of cunning intelligence to find a way (*posos*) through the problematical, and with *polytropos*, in its active sense the attribute to assume any attribute. (1990, 161)

A number of scholars have used the theme of *mētis* in valiant attempts to restore consistency to Penelope's motivations and thereby vindicate Homer's narrative skill. These scholars accept that Homer knew what he was doing when he had Penelope announce the bow contest, but they deny that her decision is a serious indication that she actually intends to remarry. She is merely deceiving the suitors, they say. For example, Philip Harsh (1950) neatly circumvents the analytic criticism of book 19 by suggesting that Penelope guesses the beggar's true identity and tacitly connives with him. This idea is still held by many and, a number of years ago, spurred hot debate on the Internet. Of those who reject the evidence for Penelope's early recognition of Odysseus as strained, there are still many who nevertheless emphasize her craftiness. In their view, the contest of the bow, like the weaving and unweaving of Laertes' shroud, is just another ruse to delay remarriage. Patricia Marquardt (1985), for example, insists that Penelope would never agree to a bride contest unless she were absolutely certain it would amount to nothing more than delay. Penelope is therefore not acting inconsistently: she is just deceiving the suitors about her real intention. This is possible, argues John Winkler (1990), because Odysseus and Penelope share essentially the same personality: both are characterized by *mētis*, skill in secrecy and lying.

Disguise, deception, and the manipulation of reality are undeniably central concerns of the *Odyssey*, and any approach that does not account for these is seriously flawed. There are, however, problems with the assumption that the signal virtue of one forceful character, even the eponymous hero, ought to be imitated by the other main characters. Why should we not expect Homer to use Penelope as a challenge to the very theme of *mētis* rather than as an example of it? Furthermore, Penelope is doomed to prove inferior in *mētis* to Odysseus on any conceivable scale. How could she compete in wile with the wiliest of humans? Her deceits, no matter how amplified, are but a candle to his bonfire. Worst of all, the assumption that Penelope is lying about her own motives has become an open invitation to read into her mind

6

motivations that are not hers or to disregard those that are. If we are allowed to pronounce her statements as false when we have no evidence from either her or the narrator that they are, we are free to discount or distort everything she says. Her yes becomes no; her no becomes yes. This will not do.

One approach promoted by feminists in the last fifteen years partly avoids the temptation to put words in Penelope's mouth. This approach, which has itself profited greatly from the work on *mētis*, eagerly embraces the postmodernist virtue of indeterminacy. It does not insist that Penelope is always lying; rather, it holds that we can never be certain whether she is or not. Ioanna Papadopoulou-Belmehdi finds Penelope "*insaissisable*," (elusive) continually woven and unwoven like "*la toile irrationnelle*" (the irrational web) that supposedly symbolizes her (1994, 87). Nancy Felson-Rubin, in her book *Regarding Penelope: From Character to Poetics* (1994) and in her article "Penelope's Perspective: Character from Plot" (1996), deconstructs Penelope's agency by presenting a character that, according to her, is enmeshed in any number of diverse subplots and themes. Thus, Penelope's motives seem contradictory to us only because of our inability to determine what she is trying to accomplish at any one moment. Marilyn Katz goes further. In *Penelope's Renown: Meaning and Indeterminacy in Homer's "Odyssey"* (1997), Katz argues that indeterminacy is the very nature of Penelope's character and that, therefore, by definition, her motivations cannot be fathomed. Sheila Murnaghan, in *Disguise and Recognition in the "Odyssey"* (1987a), locates Homer's very genius in his lack of narrative specificity and his refusal to settle for purposeful motivations. According to her, Homer is trying to emphasize that in real life, the final word belongs to chance or even absurdity. While it is true that indeterminacy may well reflect a reader's or an audience's uncertainty as a story unfolds, the presumption of indeterminacy falls short for my purposes here. It tends to render Penelope's character either too passive or too trivial.

The last approach I shall mention here is perhaps really more of a fundamental assumption underlying all previous approaches. The assumption is that Penelope is to be understood in terms of her sexual fidelity to Odysseus. This is a very old idea. In the *Heroides*, Ovid portrays Penelope as completely dependent on her husband and obsessed with their romantic bond. Ovid imagines that Penelope writes to Odysseus and promises, "Tua sum, tua dicar oportet; Penelope coniunx semper Vlixis ero" [I am yours. I must be called yours. Penelope will always be Ulysses' wife].⁴ The idea has endured. Penelope continues to be praised or blamed principally for her sexual conduct. Many readers still believe that the only thing she can do wrong is to embrace a man other than Odysseus. Such readers are therefore bitterly disappointed with her for what seems to be her dangerous flirtation with remarriage when she announces that the competition of the bow will be a contest for her hand. In his article "Wise Penelope and the Contest of the Bow" (1983), Combellack complains: "Penelope, the model of cautious, shrewd intelligence, acts on this one occasion like a rash, precipitate fool. It is quite understandable that Homer's readers have often wondered why" (111). That attitude is of the sort that invites strong reactions, like Wendy Helleman's when she asserts in her article "Homer's Penelope: A Tale of Feminine Arete," "Twenty years of single-minded loyalty and patient waiting for a missing husband would certainly appear to be rather much to expect of a beautiful, young and clever woman with wealth and property at her disposal" (1995a, 229).

Froma Zeitlin has attempted to deflect disdain for Penelope by turning the tables in the sexual power struggle. In 1995, Zeitlin wrote that Penelope's testing of Odysseus's identity in book 23 "raises the far more important question of *her* sexual fidelity to him," and Zeitlin calls this "the principal anxiety that hovers over the whole poem" (122). The trouble with accepting that Penelope's power is restricted to the sexual realm is that it affords her little claim to exceptionality. Instead of turning the eyes of the suitors, which she does reluctantly and with the occasional aid of Athene, Penelope prefers solitude and a chance to grieve for her lost husband. Comparison to any number of other female figures in the *Odyssey* makes her appear embarrassingly passive. Thus, misogyny and feminism can find a strange, if not inevitable, conjunction in Charles Boer's evaluation.

> Not that one has much sympathy for [Penelope], in her dopey narcoleptic trances falling asleep every few minutes when a crisis occurs—this may be how Mediterranean men fantasize their wives really are when they're away, and what they want them to be like—but, no thanks Molly Bloom, we'll take Helen any day over the dizzy housewife.⁵

Innovations in the study of the *Odyssey* cannot be denied. Deception as a major theme, the complexity and self-consciousness of narrative technique, an emphasis on indeterminacy, the awareness that the *Odyssey* comprises many additions to its earliest version—none of these am I inclined to deny. As productive as they have been, however, they have involved fundamental assumptions that inherently tend to maximize the passivity of Penelope's character and to minimize the importance of the events in Ithaca. In an attempt to use what is useful in them to illuminate Penelope's agency while at the same time bracketing (in the sense that Husserl used the word in his *Cartesian Meditations*) their prejudicial assumptions, I have laid down a few principles for my own study. (1) I shall treat the text as an integral whole. (2) I shall assume that any additions to the text subsequent to Homer were made in a manner consistent with the direction of the plot and intent of the narrative meaning. This is to say, I shall work with the assumption, as far as possible, that Homer, or the text that we publish under his name, is competently plotted. (3) I shall assume that what is known by the characters in the narrative must be rigorously distinguished from what is known by the narratee to whom the story is being told. Therefore, (4) I will abandon the notion (fairly widespread even among contemporary commentators) that any of the characters can or should speak for the narrator. Finally, (5) I shall assume that Penelope gives accurate accounts of her own feelings and motives.

This last principle is likely to be the most controversial. I do not mean to say that Penelope is incapable of deceit or that she ought to be. Certainly, she lies. Before the moment when the *Odyssey* opens, she has deceived the suitors for three years with her weaving. In book 23, she tells a lie about her bed, or she at least promotes the false impression that it has been hacked from its foundation. Nevertheless, in both cases of lying, the epic audience has (or soon gets) independent proof of the truth. The same holds true for all of Odysseus's lies. I am not calling for treating Penelope and Odysseus differently; in fact, I insist on employing the same criterion for evaluating the truth of what each says. Every time Odysseus lies, the epic audience knows that he is lying. Conversely, when there is no evidence that Odysseus is lying, we readily accept his account about his feelings or thoughts. For example, no one doubts that he is eager to return home, is happy to embrace his son, is touched by Argos's loyalty, or intends to take revenge on the suitors. In contrast, nearly everything that Penelope reports about herself is brought into question by critics of the text. Winkler, for instance, writes about Penelope's famous dream of the twenty geese in book 19, "Though Penelope does have dreams in the Odyssey, I see no reason to believe that she actually had this dream" (1990, 153). One cannot help but feel that Winkler's skepticism is a result of the difficulty he has fitting her dream into his interpretation. In a like manner, Penelope is conveniently supposed to be deceitful when she reports anything about herself. So, Penelope is thought to be lying when she says that she is all out of ways to stall the suitors; that Odysseus gave her a clear injunction about his wishes when he left; that she intends to follow this injunction; that she believes Odysseus will probably never return home; that she has decided to remarry; that she means for the bow contest to select her a husband; that she does not recognize the Cretan as Odysseus until she gives him the test of the bed; and that her testing of Odysseus was motivated by fear of being tricked by an impostor. Some of these claims have been denied by virtually all critics; all of them have been denied by some. But the narrative offers no grounds for thinking any of these to be deceptions.

This book asserts that Penelope offers strikingly accurate and straightforward accounts of her own feelings, intentions, and beliefs and that all of them square with the logic of the narrative. In the pages that follow, I will offer evidence—intended to persuade the skeptic—of the sincerity of Penelope's various reports about what she thinks and feels. I will also argue that the possible alternatives to her announced intentions either are untenable or are destructive to her interests or to the integrity of the plot. However, my main loyalty is to those who are willing to grant Penelope the right to speak for herself and are willing to listen to what she says. Thus, I see the major importance of this work not in the polemic about whether Penelope is lying at this or that moment but, rather, in the light that is shed on the plot, the characters, and the theme of the Odyssey when Penelope is taken at her word.

CHAPTER ONE

The Stakes of the Plot

In *On The Sublime*, Longinus judges the *Odyssey* to be clearly inferior to the *Iliad*, on the grounds that the former appears less dramatic and vivid. The 1996 edition of the *Oxford Classical Dictionary* seems to agree: "The *Odyssey* is a romance, enjoyable at a more superficial level than the heroic/tragic *Iliad*" (718). Longinus rejects plot unity in the *Odyssey* out of hand: he thinks that the aging Homer not only loses his edge but his direction as well. "Henceforth we see the ebbing tide of Homer's greatness, as he wanders in the incredible regions of romance" (9.13). The *OCD* echoes, "For many readers the adventures are the high point" (719). In fact, many school editions of the epic (e.g., Herbert Bates's otherwise admirable 1969 translation) altogether exclude the Telemachy and other "slow" parts and begin with Odysseus weeping on the Ogygian shore. This approach is not restricted to editors of school editions. Peter Brooks, in his 1992 *Reading for the Plot: Design and Intention in Narrative*, writes, "The *Iliad* opens with Agamemnon and Achilles locked in passionate quarrel over the girl Briseis, and the *Odyssey* with Odysseus, detained on Calypso's island, expressing the longing of his *nostos*, the drive to return home" (38). Of course, the *Odyssey* does not open on the Ogygian shore; the tale takes us first to Olympus and then to Ithaca. Moreover, it does not open at a moment particularly significant in the tale of Odysseus's *nostos*.

Why does the *Odyssey* begin when and where it does, in Ithaca, in the twentieth year after the beginning of the Trojan campaign? One who takes the *Odyssey* primarily as a *nostos* story might conceivably answer that since Ithaca is Odysseus's abiding goal, the audience ought to have an image of it to keep in mind as he journeys homeward. This is far from a satisfying answer, however, since what is currently happening in Ithaca is so unpleasant that it is more likely to undermine the goal of homecoming. Better for emphasizing the *nostos* story, I should think, would be to let the audience experience the adventures with the same idealized view of the goal that Odysseus has. This is probably why *nostos* tales, as Uvo Hölscher has shown in his analysis of folktale (1978, 1989), invariably begin with the earliest adventures of the returning hero and continue in a strict chronological order until the hero is home.

We have to put aside the idea that Homer's *Odyssey* is a traditional *nostos* story. As famous as the sea-tales that Odysseus recounts, they constitute a minor part of the poem compared to the struggles in Ithaca. Ithaca, after all, is where considerably more than half of the action takes place; Ithaca gets at least four times more attention than Scheria, the next most featured place. Furthermore, Athene elects to go to Ithaca to help Telemachos rather than to Ogygia to aid Odysseus. In fact, Athene's decision has the effect of delaying Odysseus's return. Apparently, her chief worries concern Ithaca.

As Hölscher has shown, rather than the *nostos* pattern, the beginning of the *Odyssey* conforms better to a folktale pattern sometimes called the "nick-of-time," which proceeds something like this: a departing husband specifies to his wife a limit to the time that she is supposed to wait for him before she is to consider him dead and remarry; the appointed time comes without the husband; the wedding takes its course, but the husband comes home (perhaps in disguise) just in time to prevent (or reverse) it. In the *Odyssey*, the appointed time is when the beard grows on Telemachos's chin.

Hölscher's studies have shown that Homer chose to begin the *Odyssey* in Ithaca for reasons that do not directly bear on Odysseus's *nostos*. But unfortunately, Hölscher has not solved the logical difficulties of the narrative that I discussed in my introduction. Furthermore, whereas the *Odyssey* employs the "nick-of-time" motif in the Telemachy, it distances itself from that pattern in the presentation of Penelope's weaving. As an excuse for not remarrying, the weaving of a shroud for Laertes makes very little sense. Penelope's father-in-law is old and feeble and may be near death, but the imminence of his death is emphasized only here and could easily be ignored for the purposes of the plot: no other element of the drama relies on his being moribund. A much more appropriate excuse than making a shroud for Laertes would have been making something for the impending wedding—a bridal gown, for example. The unceasing weaving and unweaving of a wedding dress ought to have been an irresistible device for a "nick-of-time" folktale. The substitution of the shroud more likely implies the hand of the poet eager to avoid, as far as possible, association with the "nick-of-time" motif and therefore with hopes for Odysseus's return. In short, the dramatic situation in Ithaca is designed not to concentrate the focus on the promise of Odysseus's return.

The question remains why the *Odyssey* begins where and when it does. Once again, Hölscher is a pioneer in the pursuit of a meaningful answer. In a 1976 lecture at the University of Cincinnati, entitled "The Transformation from Folk-Tale to Epic," he argued: "It means that the *Odyssey* starts with a crisis. Every scene of the first book is saying one thing: that the state of affairs is not to be endured any longer; that the moment has come when a decision has to be taken" (Hölscher 1978, 57). *Crisis* may be a strong word for those who hold the traditional view and insist that the basic situation in Ithaca has remained the same for many years. (This tradition is so ingrained that the entry on Penelope in the third edition of the *Oxford Classical Dictionary* mistakenly asserts that Penelope holds off the suitors by weaving and unweaving Laertes' shroud for ten years.) But crisis it is.

I part ways with Hölscher over the nature of the "state" that "is not to be endured any longer." Still looking for the folktale core, Hölscher emphasizes the romantic pressure placed on Penelope to marry, ignoring, for the most part, the struggle over the future of the House of Odysseus—a struggle without which the *Odyssey* remains the mere romance that Longinus disdained, not the agonistic drama that it might be. I agree with Agathe Thornton, who writes:

But . . . we have to change our view of the *Odyssey*: it is not a fairy story of princes competing for the hand of a beautiful queen, but it is a tale from times in which power based on wealth and brute force was little hampered by law, a tale of greedy and ambitious aristocrats trying under a thin veneer of courtliness to seize the absent king's wife, wealth and position. (1970, 67)

To know what is really going on in Ithaca and what counts in the structure of the plot, we must take a careful look at the epic's generally neglected second book. It delineates a power struggle in which the principal agents are the Ithacans, the suitors, Telemachos, and Penelope.

TELEMACHOS: ODYSSEY 2.1–14

As book 2 begins, Telemachos awakens and prepares himself to address the Ithacan assembly that he has called. To describe Telemachos, Homer here uses the same three lines that he employs to describe Menelaos in book 4. Like that triumphant hero, the young man cuts a godlike figure.

> [He] put on his clothes, and slung a sharp sword over his
>   shoulder.
> Underneath his shining feet he bound the fair sandals
> and went on his way from the chamber, like a god in presence.
>
> (*Od.* 2.3–5)

Telemachos will cut a very different figure by the end of book 2, but here the Ithacan people "marvel at the young hero" as he strides into the assembly, spear in hand, with a couple of fine hounds at his side and with Athene's enchanting grace glowing forth from his whole person. The elders make room for him, and the epic audience is set to expect great and noble words.

AIGYPTIOS: ODYSSEY 2.15–34

The first to speak is not Telemachos but one of the Ithacan citizens, "the hero Aigyptios, who was bent over with age, and had seen things beyond number" (*Od.* 2.15–16). His first words reveal that there has been no official assembly in Ithaca for twenty years—that is, since Odysseus left. "Never has there been an assembly of us or any session since great Odysseus went away in the hollow vessels" (2.26–27). This means that Telemachos has never before convened a public assembly. In fact, Telemachos's public life has been so slight that Aigyptios cannot even guess that Telemachos might be behind the call.

So who has been ruling Ithaca? The answer is no one. Odysseus did once, as "king," when he was in Ithaca, but since then, apparently no one has taken his place. There has not even been any official public discussion of the matter. Ithaca has therefore been more or less in anarchy for twenty years, a system that seems to have worked tolerably well for everyone. I think we can figure that each Ithacan household has reverted to the ancient practice of taking care of itself. Aigyptios's own family, consisting of his four sons, reflects a balance of interests in regard to the House of Odysseus. Two of his sons have involvement with it, one as a friend and one as an enemy. Antiphos sailed with Odysseus to Troy; Eurynomos is a suitor. The other two sons (unnamed, as are all of the unaffiliated Ithacans except Aigyptios) are at home, minding their familial estates (2.22). If we take Aigyptios's family as representative of the interests of the Ithacan populace, we see that Telemachos is about to address an assembly of men with complex, balanced affiliations that are dominated by private pursuits. Most of them have been doing just fine and will continue to do so if nothing changes.

Aigyptios assumes that this rare public assembly has been called because of some public emergency. He proclaims goodwill for anyone ready to shoulder public concerns and aid the community at large. Even before he knows the identity of the one who has convened the assembly, he offers his approval and endorsement: "I think he is a good man and useful. So may Zeus grant him good accomplishment for whatever it is his mind desires" (2.33–34). This enthusiastic endorsement is highly ironic within the context of the *Odyssey*. The accomplishment of Telemachos's desires will prove a curse to Aigyptios, who still grieves over the loss of his first son: "he could not forget the lost one. He grieved and mourned for him, and it was in tears for him, now, that he stood forth and addressed [the assembly]" (2.23–24). Aigyptios's second son will die along with the other suitors.[1]

Telemachos takes Aigyptios's words as support and encouragement but immediately acts in a way to render them inapplicable. Aigyptios has praise and appreciation for anyone who warns against invasion "or has some other public matter to set forth and argue" (2.32), but not for one like Telemachos, who has come to request help, not to offer it. Though urgent, Telemachos's business is a private matter, a mere personal need. Mutatis mutandis, Telemachos's line is an echo of Aigyptios's, but in the negative: "nor have I some other public matter to set forth and argue" (2.44). Aigyptios's hopes are doomed to be frustrated.

THE TWO EVILS: ODYSSEY 2.46–61

Telemachos begins to present his case. Two evils (*kaka doia*) have struck his household. First, he explains, "I have lost a noble father, one who was king once over you here, and was kind to you like a father" (*Od.* 2.46–47).[2] The statement of the first evil is bound to be surprising to the audience, who has witnessed, not long before, the opening scene on Olympus and therefore knows that Odysseus is not lost. But Telemachos's statement admits no equivocation. He offers no hope, warning, or threat that Odysseus might someday return home, though such a threat might have greatly aided his case against the suitors and, considering the lack of a corpse, might plausibly have been believed by the assembly.

Can Telemachos possibly believe that his father will never return? The answer is, simply, yes: he can and does. He has already announced this belief in book 1, no fewer than three times. As he first gushes out his complaints about the household to Athene, he says: "As it is, [Odysseus] has died by an evil fate, and there is no comfort left for us, not even though some one among mortals tells us he will come back. His day of homecoming has perished" (1.166–68). A little later, he says to his mother: "Odysseus is not the only one who lost his homecoming day at Troy. There were many others who perished, besides him" (1.354–55). Sixty lines later, he declares, "Eurymachos, there is no more hope of my father's homecoming" (1.413). Though Athene sends Telemachos on a long voyage to inquire about his father, she never tells him unequivocally that Odysseus is still alive. Fourteen books later, after he has absorbed many stories about his father, Telemachos levels with Theoklymenos:

> Friend, I will accurately answer all that you ask me.
> Ithaka is my country, and Odysseus is my father,
> if ever he lived; but by now he must have died by a dismal death.
>
> (15.266–68)

Telemachos's standard response to the several omens that predict his father's return is disbelief. There is no way around it: Telemachos doubts that his father is alive up until the very moment, in book 16, that the two come face-to-face.[3]

The first evil, then, is old news and is accepted as such by Telemachos and the Ithacans. (Telemachos would probably never have bothered to mention it if the second evil had not recently befallen him.) The second evil, the real cause for alarm, is the damage being done to the household by the suitors.

> [A]nd now here is a greater evil, one which presently
> will break up the whole house and destroy all my livelihood.
> For my mother, against her will, is beset by suitors.
>
> (2.48–50)

Telemachos does not deny the suitors the right to court his mother. His complaint is only that they are courting her improperly. A proper courtship would leave his inheritance intact. If the suitors are serious in their courtship, he argues, they ought to petition Ikarios, Penelope's father, for her hand. The import of these lines can hardly be exaggerated. Telemachos tacitly justifies the legitimacy of the suitors' right to court his mother. Their suit is not prima facie illegal, irreverent, or contrary to custom.

The suitors do not think that they are doing anything blamable by courting Penelope. Athene condemns them often for courting the wife of a living man, but this is an unfair charge to level at them. No one, aside from gods and prophets, claims that Odysseus is still alive. The suitors' clear conscience on this matter is most strikingly shown in the desperate defense that Eurymachos offers to Odysseus in book 22, as "each man looked about him for a way to escape sheer death" (22.43). Eurymachos does not deny that he courted Penelope, but for all that is punishable, he puts the blame on Antinoös, who, he claims, was not interested in Penelope but had other intentions.

> It was he who pushed for this action,
> not so much that he wanted the marriage, or cared for it,
> but with other things in mind, which the son of Kronos would
>   not
> grant him: to lie in wait for your son and kill him, and then
> be king himself in the district of strong-founded Ithaka.
>
> (22.49–53)

So, Telemachos claims that his mother "against her will, is beset by suitors" (2.50), but he does not claim the stronger case that the suitors have no right to court her, as they would if Odysseus were still alive. On the contrary, Telemachos wants his mother to remarry, as do Penelope's own parents (and Penelope knows that they do). Telemachos actually encourages the courtship, going so far as to reproach the suitors for laxity in their efforts. If they want Penelope so much, why have they not simply gone to her father with gifts as is customary?

> These shrink from making the journey to the house of her
>   father
> Ikarios, so that he might take bride gifts for his daughter
> and bestow her on the one he wished, who came as his
>   favorite.
>
>   (2.52–54)

Telemachos apparently assumes that Penelope's father has the authority to give away his daughter (which the father would hardly have if the husband were generally still considered alive). For their part, the suitors offer to bring their suit to Penelope's father if Telemachos will send her home, which in itself assumes that she is no longer legally bound by her marriage to Odysseus.

What peeves Telemachos the most is that the suitors' means of courtship is destroying the estate that he is due to inherit. But whose responsibility is it to protect the property? Obviously, the responsibility is Telemachos's own, in the absence of his father. Telemachos recognizes this but admits himself to be woefully inadequate to the task.

> We have no man here
> such as Odysseus was, to drive this curse from the household.
> We ourselves are not the men to do it; we must be
> weaklings in such a case, not men well seasoned in battle.
> I would defend myself if the power were in me.
>
>   (2.58–62)

TELEMACHOS'S PLEA FOR HELP: ODYSSEY 2.63–84

Telemachos can only get what he wants if the Ithacans lend him the muscle to take it. But why should they? Like Aigyptios, they have as much fealty to the suitors as they do to Telemachos. In an attempt to win them over, Telemachos serves up a gallimaufry of pleas, which become progressively less savory. I discern at least seven separate appeals, beginning with an appeal to altruism and ending with one to greed.

First, Telemachos begs for help on the grounds that his situation is no longer endurable to him (*Od.* 2.63). Second, he attempts to arouse indignation over the abuse—"beyond all decency"—of his estate (2.63–64). Third, in an attempt to shame the Ithacans into action, he says, "Even you must be scandalized and ashamed before the neighboring men about us, the people who live around our land" (2.64–66). Fourth, as if giving up on the Ithacans' sense of fair play, Telemachos attempts to tap their fear: "Fear also the god's anger lest they, astonished by evil actions, turn against you" (2.66–67). Fifth, he offers himself as a suppliant and pleads pathetically, "leave me alone with my bitter sorrow to waste away" (2.70–71). He thereby methodically undercuts his own best argument for the intensity of the evil that has befallen him and for the urgency of his need.

As if this were not enough, Telemachos's sixth strategy involves insulting the Ithacans. He implies that they have gone well beyond mere toleration of the suitors, that they, in fact, are the very ones who incited the suitors and instigated the attack on his property (2.73–74). Finally, Telemachos follows this up with a cynical appeal to greed (2.74–79). He suggests that the Ithacans cut out the suitors as middlemen and snatch all his property for themselves. That way, he says, he might one day have some chance of getting it back. Better to be robbed by thieves that cannot run too far. If anything, Telemachos has now sunk below the low moral standards of which he has just been accusing the Ithacans themselves. That the Ithacans do not take him up on his offer or race each other to loot the palace becomes a tribute to their basic honesty and reminds us that they are not as Telemachos portrays them.

The fall from the heroic opening lines is precipitous. Telemachos ends up presenting himself as an extremely callow and pathetic character, reduced to ineffectual and adolescent anger: "So he spoke in anger, and dashed to the ground the scepter in a stormburst of tears" (2.80–81). The Ithacans are silent, like those who hear a riveting story with a bad turn. They are unsure how to react. They seem to feel that the most proper response to the implicit insults and attacks would be angry words of their own. But no one dares. It is not, of course, that they are afraid of Telemachos but that he seems too fragile, too near the breaking point.

THE SUITORS' COUNTERSUIT: *ODYSSEY* 2.85–128

Antinoös, the ringleader of the suitors, takes the floor to present their case. He admits that the courtship has gone awry, but he puts the blame squarely and solely on Penelope. Pieced together from Antinoös's account, the chronicle of events seems to run as follows. For nearly four years, at least, the suitors have had a desire for Penelope to marry one of them.[4] The trouble began early on, when Penelope began "denying the desires of the Achaians" (2.90), who began to feel cheated. At or about this time, she made clear her intentions. She admitted Odysseus's death and promised—tacitly, if not explicitly—to remarry. She sent out—or continued to send out—secret messages of encouragement to all the suitors individually: "For she holds out hope to all, and makes promises to each man" (2.91). Nevertheless, she requested a delay before she chose the man—enough time, she contended, to do her duty by her father-in-law, who would need a burial shroud when he dies. This is the famous weaving trick that is recounted three times in the *Odyssey*. The suitors consented and considered themselves rather gallant for doing so: "and the proud heart in us was persuaded" (2.103). The weaving went on for more than three years before the suitors discovered that Penelope had been cheating them, unweaving at night whatever she had woven by day. When the suitors eventually caught her, they compelled her to finish the shroud. They were not, however, able to compel her to choose a husband.

The question of how much actual power the suitors have over Penelope is complex and is fundamental to understanding the structure of the conflicts in the *Odyssey*. Telemachos says that his mother is beset by suitors "against her will" and that the suitors can and will force her to marry. Yet we must confront complaints, like those from Denys Page, that the suitors do not exercise the power that they have. Page accuses Homer of a serious lapse of narrative competency when the suitors neglect to force Penelope to marry once she has finished the shroud.

[F]or it would surely be a sad story-teller, who told us that Penelope was caught unpicking the web and compelled to finish it, and yet that nothing whatever happened as a consequence— that the Suitors generously regarded the incident as closed, and allowed affairs to continue exactly as they were before the story of the web began. But that is what actually happens in the *Odyssey*. . . . (1955, 120–21)

The suitors are not acting generously. Rather, they are applying as much pressure as they can manage. If they do not go farther, it is because their power is checked by the power that the Ithacan populace itself wields.

It is an overlooked—if strange—fact that the structure of power between the protagonists and the mass of unnamed common people is more significant in the *Odyssey* than in the *Iliad*. Though the setting of the *Iliad* is either the crowded Greek camp, bustling Troy, or the battlefield, the Greek or Trojan populace has little or no influence on the direction of the plot, and their leaders do not expect them to claim any. The poet gives them flighty emotions and no backbone. Thersites, thoroughly dominated and humiliated by Odysseus, is the symbol of their role. In the *Odyssey*, in contrast, each party thinks that having the populace on its side would ensure its success; but the populace is sternly independent. Each party is also afraid that a mistake on its part will push the populace over to the other side. Furthermore, it seems that solid moral standards guide Ithacan opinion. Telemachos is afraid of popular resentment if he sends his mother away. The suitors are afraid of popular retaliation if they are caught hurting Telemachos. Once home, Odysseus also assumes that the Ithacan populace will be a force to reckon with. He asks Athene how he will escape even if he kills all the suitors. The implication is that the Ithacans will not tolerate his action. From book 24, we know that this is a fact. No one seems to have any confusion about the popular Ithacan response. The people are not to be easily manipulated. Theirs is a solid and primal sense of justice. They would rise up equally against the killers of Telemachos as against the murderer of the suitors.

Telemachos's claim that Penelope is being courted against her will is not in any way a moral accusation. How unwilling can Penelope be and still hold out hope to the suitors? Anything to which she does not consent would probably be much resented by her own parents and would certainly not be sanctioned by the Ithacans. Furthermore, the suitors need Penelope to choose one of them. If the choice is not hers, I think it would be impossible for the suitors to decide among themselves who would carry her away and who would go home disappointed. If it were possible simply to carry off an unwilling Penelope, as if by the hair, someone probably would have already done so.

Like Telemachos, Antinoös ends by implicating the Ithacans. Unlike Telemachos, he makes a point that the Ithacans cannot deny:
Penelope is increasing her *kleos*, and the Ithacans are helping her.
The townspeople esteem Penelope in direct proportion to her obstinate fidelity to the memory of Odysseus (as many modern readers of
the epic do as well). Several sources reveal that this is the opinion of
the Ithacan populace. In his very next speech in book 2, when he
gives the culminating reason not to send Penelope home to her father,
Ikarios, Telemachos cites the fact that the Ithacans would resent him
for it (*Od.* 2.136–37). Penelope, in book 19, reveals Ithacan expectations when she wonders whether she should continue to live in a way
that would please the people or whether she should remarry and leave
her house (19.524–29). Finally, the Ithacans speak for themselves in
book 23. We overhear them speculating, outside the barred doors of
the palace, that Penelope has disappointed them by accepting a new
husband (23.148–51). To them, Penelope is most admirable if she resists marriage. Antinoös seems to know this, since he does not ask for
direct intervention from the Ithacans: he merely asks them to stay out
of the way.

What is left to the suitors if they cannot or will not use direct force
against the person of Penelope? They seem to believe that they have
but one alternative. If Penelope cannot be directly pressured as a
woman, she can be indirectly pressured as a mother. Therefore, the
suitors have quite consciously resolved to do just what Telemachos is
complaining about. They intend to waste the estate until either there
is nothing left of it or Penelope chooses a new husband. Their hope is
that the mother will capitulate to pressure from her son or will buckle
under the weight of her own guilt over depriving her son of his rightful inheritance and destroying his future prospects. "So long, I say, will
your livelihood and possessions be eaten away, as long as she keeps this
purpose, one which the very gods, I think, put into her heart" (2.123–
25). This is a united front. Later, Eurymachos, in his speech, echoes
the strategy: "there will not be compensation, ever, while she makes
the Achaians put off marriage with her" (2.203–5).

One of the most important implications of this sequence is that
the suitors have only recently begun their war of attrition against the
House of Odysseus. There are many reasons for thinking so. Before
Penelope began to frustrate their marital hopes, the suitors had no in-
centive for squandering an estate that they hoped to acquire them-

selves. (In fact, the suitors seem mainly to have offered hospitality to Telemachos in their own homes.)[5] It is unlikely that they were pursuing this strategy during the three years that Penelope resorted to the trick of the web. Until the suitors caught Penelope at her trick, they had no reason to antagonize the woman whom each hoped would choose him to wed and from whom each was getting secret, personal encouragements. Besides, Penelope's trick of the web becomes much less effective—if not self-destructive—with the suitors in residence. Even if we assume that Odysseus's wealth (poor, compared to that of the kings of the mainland cities) could have supported the suitors for so long, what good would Penelope draw from giving them carte blanche to waste it? Also, what good would the suitors' strategy of attrition do them if Penelope has already proved impervious to it? One would even expect Telemachos, far from giving up his cause just after Eurymachos complains about having been forced to waste so much time on false promises, to have simply reminded Eurymachos that he had been paid well for those years. Furthermore, Telemachos says that he was alerted to the threat to his property only some little time before Athene's epiphany. If he had ignored that fact for three years, he would perhaps be as culpable as the suitors—and much more stupid. In short, the only sequence of events that involves no logical or narratological contradictions is one in which the suitors' strategy of attrition is started after Penelope is caught cheating and still refuses to pick a husband, even though the shroud is complete.

TELEMACHOS'S ANSWER: ODYSSEY 2.129–45

The suitors' strategy is aimed at Penelope. It is never intended to force Telemachos's hand directly or even to get him to do what it claims to ask of him. Though Antinoös pretends to urge Telemachos to return Penelope to her father, the suitors apparently neither want nor expect Telemachos to do anything of the kind. They seem as reluctant as Telemachos to involve Ikarios. After all, as Telemachos points out, the suitors could ask Ikarios for his daughter's hand on their own account, even in Penelope's absence. Thus, Antinoös seems to make his demand knowing full well how unthinkable it is for Telemachos, who, in fact, rejects it promptly in his next speech: "Antinoös, I cannot thrust the mother who bore me, who raised me, out of the house against her will" (*Od.* 2.130–31).

His reasons are not very high-minded and mainly involve concern for his own personal and financial security. Sending Penelope away, he worries, would incur a great expense (presumably because her dowry would go back with her) as well as retaliation from the wronged parties—Penelope's father, Penelope herself, and the Ithacan people.

> It will be hard
> to pay back Ikarios, if willingly I dismiss my mother.
> I will suffer some evil from her father, and the spirit will give
>   me
> more yet, for my mother will call down her furies upon me
> as she goes out of the house, and I shall have the people's
> resentment.
>
>   (2.132–37)

Telemachos ends by saying, "I will not be the one to say that word to her" (2.137). He thus leaves open the possibility that he would not oppose the one who did. For their part, however, the suitors have no intention of playing that role, and they do not blink when Telemachos effetely insists that if they are not happy with his demands, they can just go home. Telemachos lacks the heart to brave either of his options—repatriate his mother or fight the suitors. He is reduced to threatening to call on Zeus for aid, though his threat seems pathetically weakened by the word *somehow*: "I will cry out to the gods everlasting in the hope that Zeus might somehow grant a reversal of fortunes" (2.143–44).

THE SPEECHES OF HALITHERSES AND
EURYMACHOS: ODYSSEY 2.146–223

To everyone's surprise, two eagles suddenly appear in the sky. They fly companionably together until they reach the assembly. Then,

> they turned on each other suddenly in a thick shudder
> of wings, and swooped over the heads of all, with eyes glaring
> and deadly, and tore each other by neck and cheek with their
>   talons.
>
>   (*Od.* 2.151–53)

"This," says West, "is the commonest type of omen in Homer, and the interpretation is invariably easy" (1988, 141). The Ithacans, however, are less sure of its meaning: "Then all were astounded at the birds, when their eyes saw them, and they pondered in their hearts over what might come of it" (*Od.* 2.155–56).

Taking the floor, Halitherses offers his interpretation, construing the omen in a way that is congenial and not at all surprising to us, the external audience, who have been privy to the Olympian council described in book 1. Halitherses prophesies that Odysseus is still alive and will soon be on his way home (2.163–66). The prophecy does not impress the Ithacans. Nor should it, really. After all, as fictional characters and members of the audience internal to the narrative, they do not enjoy the advantage of knowing what we, the external audience, know. The narrator, who endorses Halitherses' skill to us, does not speak to them. They are left merely with Halitherses' self-promotional claim: "I who foretell this am not untried, I know what I am saying" (2.170). Halitherses offers no recent or conclusive examples of his skill. He gives only one old and wholly inadequate example.

> Concerning [Odysseus], I say that everything was accomplished
> in the way I said it would be at the time the Argives took ship
> for Ilion, and with them went resourceful Odysseus.
> I said that after much suffering, with all his companions
> lost, in the twentieth year, not recognized by any,
> he would come home. And now all this is being accomplished.
> (2.171–76)

His argument is essentially this: "The fact that I so clearly foresaw an event through the gloom of twenty long years ought to prove to you that I can easily discern this same event when it is just around the corner."

The force of the narrative is to pull the audience in two directions. We who know of the council on Olympus know that Halitherses' prediction is substantially right, if not entirely accurate.[6] At the same time, we cannot reasonably expect any levelheaded Ithacan to accept Halitherses' specious logic.

Eurymachos, the next suitor to speak, impugns the prophet's motive and method. First, he makes a cogent, general point about the interpretation of natural signs. Not all things, he argues, are meaningful simply because we wish them to be: "Many are the birds who under the sun's rays wander the sky; not all of them mean anything" (2.181–82).

Next, he attacks Halitherses for offering his accommodating prophecy with an eye to personal profit. Eurymachos then offers his own prediction, which, given Telemachos's psychology and the hostility that his current demands have aroused in the suitors, has a certain ring of wisdom.

> But I will tell you straight out, and it will be a thing
>   accomplished:
> if you, who know much and have known it long, stir up a
>   younger
> man, and by talking him round with words encourage his
>   anger,
> then first of all, it will be the worse for him; he will not
> on account of all these sayings be able to accomplish anything.
>
> (2.187–91)

Though less prophecy, perhaps, than threat, Eurymachos's words constitute a more plausible account of future facts. Kindling the impotent anger of Telemachos will only ignite the potent wrath of the suitors. Eurymachos would fain portray the suitors as Telemachos's real protectors: "And on you, old sir, we shall lay a penalty, and it will grieve your mind as you pay it, and that for you will be a great sorrow" (2.192–93). Eurymachos's advice that Telemachos obey the suitors, though, is quickly backed up by more unconditional demands and threats of force. He then restates the grim purpose of their strategy of attrition: "[Telemachos's] possessions will be wretchedly eaten away, there will not be compensation, ever, while [Penelope] makes the Achaians put off marriage with her" (2.203–5).

Like Antinoös, Eurymachos ends his speech with the insistence that the suitors are really Penelope's victims, and he even adds more plausibility to the argument. By stringing the suitors along with her delays and tricks, he claims, Penelope has wasted their valuable time and prevented them from wooing other desirable young women as their brides.

> . . . while we, awaiting this, all our days
> quarrel for the sake of her excellence, nor ever go after
> others, whom any one of us might properly marry.
>
> (2.205–7)

By implication, private Ithacan families with daughters of marriageable age are also paying the price of Penelope's dilatory tactics.

Howard Clarke's judgment intended to describe Telemachos in book 1 rings true here as well: "Athena's encouragement is not without its effect, but Telemachus' adolescent attempts to take charge are a fiasco" (1969, 29). All of a sudden, Telemachos drops his plea, as if finally recognizing that he can make no headway in this manner without the support of the Ithacans. He contents himself with announcing that he wants to go away on a voyage to Sparta and Pylos to learn what has happened to his father. Even here, the young man's essential resourcelessness is painfully evident: he must petition the suitors to provide him with a ship and a crew.

THE SPEECHES OF MENTOR AND LEOKRITOS: ODYSSEY 2.224–59

Mentor, an old and close friend to Odysseus, intercedes in an attempt to shame the Ithacans into defending the House of Odysseus. He lays directly on the Ithacans' shoulders the blame for the suitors' excesses.

> Now it is not so much the proud suitors I resent
> . . . .
> but now I hold it against you other people, how you all
> sit there in silence, and never with an assault of words try
> to check the suitors, though they are so few, and you so many.
>
> (*Od.* 2.235–41)

Mentor's rebuke is caustic. He implies that the Ithacans are cowards. He says that they are unworthy of decent, fair, or benign rule, since obviously they respond only to force and shun the imperatives of justice. He claims that they have forgotten the legacy of Odysseus.

Mentor, of course, as an appointed caretaker of the House of Odysseus wrongly assumes that Ithacan interest corresponds to his. As we have seen, the Ithacans have other interests as well. Even the invocation of Odysseus as the gentle and benevolent leader is called into question by the text, since Odysseus proved to be a disaster for many of these families. Aigyptios's son, for example, was one of those eaten alive by the Cyclops. Nevertheless, the violence of the next speaker's response indicates a fear that Mentor's argument may have touched too close to home. Mentor was making a good point.

27

Leokritos now brazenly threatens brute force against any Ithacans who might think about taking up Telemachos's cause. He emphasizes that the suitors' strength and determination know no bounds and that none would scruple to apply brute force. Telemachos, he says, may have a couple of old men on his side, but the boy lacks all resolve and will accomplish nothing. When Leokritos abruptly cuts the assembly short, the suitors are in full control.

TELEMACHOS'S BREAK WITH THE SUITORS: ODYSSEY 2.260–320

Walking along the beach, alone and despondent, Telemachos betrays his tendency to give up altogether too easily. In his prayer to Athene, he claims that the plans she had sketched in book 1 are now thwarted by both the Achaians and the suitors. He knows himself incapable of taking the initiative in planning his own trip. Without divine intervention, he would have presumably abandoned it. But Athene, disguised now as Mentor, takes over, assuaging the young man's deepest worry by twice insisting that Telemachos is no coward.

While Athene goes off to secure a ship for the trip to the Peloponnese, Telemachos returns to his house, though still shaken. He now has a private confrontation with Antinoös, who attempts to make peace and, amazingly, removes every obstacle to Telemachos's voyage.

> Antinoös, with a smile, came straight up to Telemachos,
> and took him by the hand and spoke and named him, saying:
> "High-spoken intemperate Telemachos, now let no other
> evil be considered in your heart, neither action
> nor word, but eat and drink with me, as you did in past time.
> The Achaians will see to it that all these things are
>   accomplished,
> the ship, and chosen companions, so that you may the more
>   quickly
> reach sacred Pylos, after news about your proud father."
>
> (*Od.* 2.301–8)

It is important to understand that Antinoös is offering to reinstate a former friendliness. This means that at some time—and from Antinoös's point of view, probably to this very day—Telemachos was more or less one of the group and thought of himself that way. Antikleia, in Hades, gives independent confirmation that Telemachos and the young lords of Ithaca used to get on well (11.184–87).

Telemachos now wholly rejects the help of the suitors and all association with them. He scalds them with the anger that is "steaming up" inside him (2.315). "I will endeavor to visit evil destructions upon you, either by going to Pylos, or remaining here in the district" (2.316–17).

Is announcing an irreconcilable animus toward these desperate men a foolish move on Telemachos's part? Is Telemachos being reckless and shortsighted? I shall have more to say about these issues in chapter 3, when I investigate Telemachos's character. In any case, Telemachos never again fraternizes with the suitors except as is called for in the plan of revenge that he and Odysseus implement in the later books. I see no reason to accept George Devereux's psychoanalytic claim that an Oedipus complex renders Telemachos ambivalent about what the suitors deserve.[7]

THE SUITORS' TRUE INTENTIONS: ODYSSEY 2.321–36

Once Telemachos is off the scene, the suitors express their unguarded thoughts. We learn of the falseness of Antinoös's offer of friendship. These men have no tenderness whatsoever for Telemachos. As they prepare their dinner and move freely about the house, they mock and insult Telemachos behind his back. They maintain that as long as Telemachos is in Ithaca and under their control, he is harmless. They are aware, however, that Telemachos's intended trip to Pylos and Sparta could change everything. There, on the mainland, he might recruit reinforcements. Worse, he might obtain poison and return to kill them all by treachery.

By highlighting the threat of poison (or reinforcement), Homer preserves a delicate balance in the plot. Telemachos remains a personally undaunting figure and becomes an outsized threat only when he is allowed to leave the island. The suitors are not wrong to worry about poison. This could easily have been Athene's plan, since she describes a similar tactic used by Odysseus: "Odysseus, you see, had gone there also in his swift ship in search of a poison to kill men" (*Od.* 1.260–61). Had the thought occurred to him in Sparta, of course, Telemachos might have easily gotten the means to overpower the suitors. Menelaos declares that he had been ready to drive out the dwellers of a whole city for Odysseus (4.176), and Helen displays her pharmacological skill.

The suitors now boldly confess what they call their work. They intend to divide up all of Telemachos's possessions among themselves (though whoever succeeds in marrying Penelope will also become owner of the palace, presumably because that is something that cannot be easily divided). In short, their method is deceit, and their actual purpose is not love but theft.[8]

EURYKLEIA'S WARNING AND TELEMACHOS'S DEPARTURE: ODYSSEY 2.337–434

The scene abruptly shifts to the wide storeroom of the palace, where lie the treasures that the suitors aim to plunder.

> [Telemachos] went down into his father's high-roofed
> and wide storeroom, where gold and bronze were lying piled
>   up,
> and abundant clothing in the bins, and fragrant olive oil,
> and in it jars of wine, sweet to drink, aged,
> were standing.
>
> (*Od.* 2.337–41)

Telemachos has his nurse, Eurykleia, the incontestably loyal servant and guardian of the house, prepare his traveling provisions for him. When he confides his plans to her, she is appalled at the foolishness of the risk and aggressively tries to dissuade him from the voyage. She seems to know quite well just what the suitors intend. "And these men will devise evils against you, on your returning, so you shall die by guile, and they divide all that is yours" (2.367–68).

The final fifty-two lines of the book are devoted to the arrangements that Athene makes for the voyage. She borrows a ship and drugs the suitors into a sweet slumber. Finally, after everything is ready, she calls Telemachos to board the ship. Slipping it out of the harbor, they set sail for Pylos.

FURTHER CRISES: BEYOND BOOK 2

The first major crisis in the *Odyssey*, then, is precipitated by the suitors' change of strategy in their struggle with Penelope and places Telemachos squarely in the middle of the conflict. From this moment, the danger to Telemachos steadily intensifies. Two more crises mark its significant stages.

In book 4, as they amuse themselves nonchalantly "with discs and with light spears for throwing" (4.626), the suitors get a shock. Noëmon, the Ithacan citizen from whom Athene borrowed a ship, casually asks Antinoös whether he thinks Telemachos might have returned from Pylos yet. The suitors, who had no idea that Telemachos ever sailed, are stunned. Antinoös is beside himself with anger, as the true seriousness of the threat to his interests suddenly dawns on him. He is described as "raging, the heart within filled black to the brim with anger from beneath, but his two eyes showed like fire in their blazing" (*Od.* 4.661–62). These lines were athetized by Aristarchus because they are identical to *Iliad* 1.103–4. But reference to the *Iliad* nicely brings out the tone of this passage. Antinoös and Agamemnon feel the same way. In the *Iliad*, Calchas has just indicted Agamemnon as the cause of the devastating plague, and Agamemnon realizes that he will have to surrender Chryseis, the concubine that he loves as much as—if not more than—his lawful wife, Clytemnestra. Calchas threatens, and the Atreidean eagle prepares for attack, eyes blazing like fire.[9] One is reminded of the boar in the hunt in book 19 of the *Oydssey*.

> The thudding made by the feet of men and dogs came to him
> as they closed on him in the hunt, and against them he from
>   his woodlair
> bristled strongly his nape, and with fire from his eyes glaring
> stood up to face them close.
>
> (19.444–47)

Telemachos has brought Antinoös, the man in power, to bay—like a wild boar.

In fear that Telemachos might now topple his greedy plans, Antinoös furiously decides to ambush the boy on his way home from Pylos and to kill him.

But come now, give me a fast ship and twenty companions,
so that I can watch his return and lie in wait for him
in the narrow strait between Ithaka and towering Samos,
and make him sorry for this sea-going in search of his father.

(4.669–72)

The third crisis in the conflict between Telemachos and the suitors is forced by the failure of this ambush. In book 16, the suitors call a secret assembly and impel the next move.

We who are here must make our plans for the grim destruction
of Telemachos, so he cannot escape us; since I have no
      thought
we can get our present purpose accomplished while he is
      living.

(16.371–73)

Antinoös fears that Telemachos will report to the Ithacans and that they will be sufficiently scandalized and enraged to attack the suitors. Once again, the Ithacans are a factor in the balance of power. Antinoös has no doubt that they would be sufficient to drive him and his fellow suitors into exile.

But come now, before he can gather the Achaians and bring
      them
to assembly; for I think he will not let us go, but work out
his anger, and stand up before them all and tell them
how we designed his sudden murder, but we could not catch
      him;
and they will have no praise for us when they hear of our evil
deeds, and I fear they will work some evil on us, and drive us
from our own country, so we must make for another
      community.

(16.376–82)

Antinoös, whether sincerely or not, presents the suitors with an alternative to the assassination of Telemachos. If they are not seriously ready, he explains, to kill Telemachos and to continue with their plan to rob the boy of what he has and divide it among themselves (a plan

32

that Antinoös reiterates here), the suitors can disband and go each to his own home, courting Penelope from there with whatever expensive gifts each might manage. None of the suitors embraces this alternative except Amphinomos, who only wants to delay long enough to query the gods' will.

> We should first have to ask the gods for their counsel.
> Then, if the ordinances from great Zeus approve of it,
> I myself would kill him and tell all others to do so.
>
> (16.402–4)

Homer's plot necessitates the delay. Without it, Telemachos would be dead before he could set foot inside the palace again.

But the suitors have no intention of renouncing their plans, a fact that the poet makes emphatically clear some fifty lines later, when Eurymachos lies to Penelope, who has just heard of the plot against Telemachos's life and is demanding that the suitors give it up. Eurymachos says that "of all men Telemachos is the dearest to me by far" (16.445–46)—and there is ample evidence that of all the suitors, Eurymachos is, at least, the most friendly to Telemachos. However, after Eurymachos claims that he would never allow any harm to come to the boy, the poet adds, "So he spoke, encouraging her, but himself was planning the murder" (16.448–49).

From here on out, the death of Telemachos is merely a matter of time; that is, unless the suitors are checked by some potent force outside themselves, they will murder Penelope's son. In fact, they are on the brink of assassinating him in book 20, on the very morning that Penelope announces the bow contest—that is, on the last day of their own lives.[10]

CHAPTER TWO

Strategy for Survival

In book 1 of the *Odyssey*, Penelope descends from her upstairs chambers to make a brief and apparently rare visit to the entertainment below. Our first impression is of a retiring and fragile woman who seems willing to tolerate the invasive suitors provided that they do not indulge songs about the Trojan War, which remind her of her bitter loss.

> All in tears she spoke then to the divine singer:
> "Phemios, since you know many other actions of mortals
> and gods, which can charm men's hearts and which the singers
>   celebrate,
> sit beside them and sing one of these, and let them in silence
> go on drinking their wine, but leave off singing this sad song."
>
> (1.336–40)

Our first impression is also of someone capable of very strong feeling.

> . . . which always afflicts the dear heart deep inside me,
> since the unforgettable sorrow comes to me, beyond others,
> so dear a head do I long for whenever I am reminded
> of my husband . . .
>
> (1.341–44)

The latter part of our first impression will last. Penelope will retire to her quarters in tears of grief for her lost husband many more times before the epic is over. There is no doubt that her sorrow over Odysseus is genuine, lasting, and keen. But how accurate is the impression of fragility? In Homer, tears are not always a sign of weakness. Odysseus himself will be discovered in book 5 weeping on the Ogygian shore. Yet Telemachos encourages us to link tears with weakness when he attempts to give his mother a lesson in fortitude: "So let your heart and let your spirit be hardened to listen. Odysseus is not the only one who lost his homecoming day at Troy" (1.353–55). If others who have lost loved ones at Troy can derive pleasure from Phemios's song, perhaps it is because their feelings are less intense than Penelope's. Telemachos may be one of these. Abruptly commanding her to go back to her quarters, he adds, "For mine is the power in this household." Penelope goes without a word, "in amazement." Is Telemachos rude? Is Penelope passive? Is there tension between mother and son? Does Penelope feel less love for her son than for her husband? Though Penelope will say that her son is beloved (*agapētos*, 4.817), is this anything more than a minimum requirement for a mother? The answer to these important questions ought not to be based on this passage alone.

We do not see Penelope again for fifteen hundred lines, until, at the end of book 4, she learns of the plot against her son's life. The poetry works hard to convey the extremity of her love for him.

> So [Medon] spoke, and [Penelope's] knees gave way and the
>   heart in her.
> She stayed a long time without a word, speechless, and her
>   eyes
> filled with tears, the springing voice was held still within her.
> At long last she found words to speak to him and answer.
>
> (4.703–6)

Expressive enough on its own, the collapse of the knees and heart that is described in the first line of this passage gains force from the other nine times that it appears in Homer.[1] Each instance describes an extreme, genuine, uncontrollable emotion, usually the fear of certain—or what appears to be certain—death.[2] In the *Iliad*, a similar line describes what Lykaos feels as he faces an Achilles who has rejected all pleas for mercy (21.114). Of the seven appearances of the line in the *Odyssey*, three apply to Odysseus himself. In book 5, Odysseus feels his knees and his heart give way as he sails his little raft into the teeth of

35

the tempest that Poseidon is gathering against him (5.297). In great
fear, he says: "Ah me unhappy, what in the long outcome will befall
me? . . . My sheer destruction is certain" (5.299–305). His raft is
wrecked, and he nearly drowns. His knees and heart give way again in
fear two days later (5.406). Though the sky has cleared, the sea, still
rough, bashes him violently against the rocky Scherian coast. Had
Athene not intervened, "there his skin would have been taken off, his
bones crushed together, . . . and Odysseus would have perished,
wretched, beyond his destiny" (5.426–36). As it is, he leaves some of
his skin on the rocks. In book 22, when he is in battle against the overwhelming numbers of suitors who have managed to arm themselves,
Odysseus feels his knees and heart giving way one last time (22.147).
In turn, the suitors feel their own give way when they first realized that
Odysseus, who has just jugulated Antinoös with an arrow, intends to
slaughter all the rest of them as well (22.68).

The use of this formula for Penelope shows that she feels the threat
to her son as a mortal threat to herself. In fact, thirty lines later, she
will tell Eurykleia that she would have laid down her life to prevent
Telemachos from departing, from placing himself at risk (4.734). The
poet embroiders upon the point in the famous simile that compares
Penelope to a lion at bay (4.791–92). Of course, the suitors have no intention of killing Penelope, but the narrator signals that Penelope
would defend Telemachos's life with her own.

At the moment, Penelope's very breath seems to be arrested, as fear
for her son floods her heart. "She stayed a long time without a word,
speechless, and her eyes filled with tears, the springing voice was held
still within her" (4.704–5). To an ear attuned to both epics, this pair
of lines plucks the memory of its companion at *Iliad* 17.695–96, which
is identical and repeated nowhere else.[3] In the *Iliad*, the pair of lines
describes how Antilochus reacts to devastating news: Hector has killed
Patroklos and kept Achilles' armor, and as if that were not enough,
Menelaos, who is now quite certain that the Trojans will crush the
Greeks, is commanding Antilochus to report the news to Achilles. As
hair-raising as the prospect of reporting such news to the brooding hero
must have been, Antilochus is not paralyzed. "Yet even so," as the poet
goes on to say, "he neglected not Menelaos' order but went on the run"
(*Il.* 17.697–98).

Penelope's consternation goes deeper and is not so easily dispelled.

It is a long time before she can collect herself enough to talk. "At long last she found words to speak to him and answer" (*Od.* 4.706). Compare Odysseus on his voyage from Ogygia. The storm hurls him underwater, and for a long time, he is unable to come up for air because of the weight of the clothes that Calypso has given him—and no doubt we are supposed to feel it as a very long while indeed (we hold our breath, you may say, to our limits). But he finally resurfaces, spitting out the bitter brine. Penelope, too, her face streaming with tears, eventually finds her voice. When she does, she manages to ask Medon why Telemachos has put himself in such mortal danger. The answer overwhelms her.

> And a cloud of heart-wasting sorrow was on her, she had no
> strength left
> to sit down in a chair, though there were many there in the
> palace,
> but sat down on the floor of her own well-wrought
> bedchamber weeping pitifully.
>
> (4.716–19)

It may be hard for modern readers to appreciate the extremity of a grief that would cause a Homeric queen to disregard the great indignity of sitting on the floor. Odysseus, it is true, sits on the floor on three occasions; but this is the disguised Odysseus, who, as a dirty, ragged beggar, is purposely assigned the lowest possible place of seating. Even then, his placement is a sign of inhospitality: the floor is for indigents or animals—or for one so distraught as to forget all dignity, comfort, status, or propriety.

Penelope loses awareness of bodily needs as well: she neither eats nor drinks.

> [She] lay there fasting, she had tasted no food nor drink, only
> pondering whether her stately son would escape from dying
> or have to go down under the hands of the insolent suitors.
>
> (4.788–90)

The only other character in the *Odyssey* who goes without food or drink in this way is Laertes, when he, in his turn, learns that Telemachos is in mortal danger.

[T]hey say he has not eaten in this way, nor drunk anything,
nor looked to his farm, but always in lamentation and
    mourning
sits grieving, and the flesh on his bones is wasting from him.

(16.143–45)

In order that we should not think that this is a routine or common reaction to sorrow, Homer tells us that Laertes, as distraught as he has
been about Odysseus's absence, never before went this far in his grief.

. . . [H]e so greatly grieved for Odysseus
yet would look after his farm and with the thralls in his
    household
would eat and drink, whenever the spirit was urgent with him. . .

(16.139–41)

The *Odyssey* is an epic that celebrates eating and drinking. Hunger is
normally intolerable, as when Odysseus's men cannot resist roasting the
sacred cattle of the Sun, though they know it will cost them their lives.

Is this enough to convince us that Penelope's consternation over
the threat to her son is all-consuming? I am inclined to think so. But
Homer goes further by bringing in an "outside" authority.[4] Penelope
makes a desperate prayer to Athene, and Athene becomes sufficiently
alarmed to feel that she must intervene. She sends an image of Iphthime, Penelope's sister, in a dream, to ease the suffering that has left
Penelope teetering at the brink of the intolerable.

Then in turn the dark dream image spoke to her in answer:
"Take courage, let not your heart be too altogether frightened,
such an escort goes along with him, and one that other
men would have prayed to have standing beside them, for she
    has power,
Pallas Athene, and she has pity on you in your grieving,
and it is she who has sent me to you to tell you of these
    things."

(4.824–29)

As an authority, Athene ought to be able to impress the most hard-
bitten cynic. The goddess who could abandon her favorite hero for ten

troubling years is no soft touch. This is the only time that she offers Penelope any information whatsoever about her plans. Furthermore, from the point of view of simple plot construction, Athene's intervention is strange. Considering that the threat to Telemachos is meant to be a real one and to hang like a pall over the whole of the next ten books—in fact, Athene will try to frighten Zeus with the prospect of it at the second council on Olympus—would it not seem more exciting to hold Penelope (and the audience with her) in suspense about Telemachos's safety?

The only reasonable explanation for this scene—which holds an absolutely salient position in the *Odyssey*, in that it is the very last scene before the poet switches his attention to Odysseus—is the signal importance of understanding the power of Penelope's love for her son, a love that is utterly unqualified. Athene's alarm confirms what every attentive reader has begun to suspect: Odysseus is not Penelope's chief concern. So, we have every reason to take her seriously when she tells the image of her sister, "And it is for [Telemachos] I grieve even more than for [Odysseus]" (4.819).

Penelope does, in fact, take the opportunity to ask about Odysseus after she has heard the good news about her son. But Iphthime treats it as an idle question. Unlike the news about Telemachos, Athene thinks that Penelope can live without knowing that Odysseus is alive. The rebuff is certainly not welcome news, but it does not ruffle Penelope, who awakes "soothed in the inward heart, because this clear dream in the dim of night had come to visit her" (4.840–41). There is no limit to her joy, as there surely would be if she were hanging onto hopes for Odysseus's return.

THE HOUSE OF ODYSSEUS

Telemachos's physical safety is not Penelope's only worry. If it were, she herself might have sent him away to the Peloponnese or even farther before this. She certainly would not be so distraught over the fact that her son has gone to the Peloponnese. After all, he is safest when he has no contact with the suitors. Her words imply a deeper worry: "Must it be so that even his name shall be gone from men's minds?" (*Od.* 4.710). This is a worry that finds temporary calm only when Eurykleia assures her by saying:

I think the seed of Arkeisios is not altogether hated
by the blessed gods, but there will still be one left to inherit
the high-roofed house and the rich fields that lie at a distance.

(4.754–57)

What Penelope wants is not just for Telemachos to live but for him
to reach maturity, to successfully claim and preserve the inheritance
that is due to him, and, by so doing, to continue the family line—that
is, to preserve the *oikos*. I here use the term *oikos* in the broadest sense,
to include the palace, fields, household goods, and other possessions
that are to be passed down to subsequent generations in an unbroken
line. The closest English term is probably *entailed estate*. What I call
"the House of Odysseus," then, is the entailed estate passed down from
Arkeisios to Laertes and from Laertes to Odysseus. It is Telemachos's
inheritance as well as his legacy. Let us look at its two basic elements
in turn, the possessions and the lineage.[5]

Tangible riches command open respect in the *Odyssey* to a degree
that can embarrass modern scholars. Odysseus, sacker of cities, un-
abashedly pursues treasures to increase the wealth of his house. Several
times, he cites it as an acceptable explanation for staying so long away
from home. In the same spirit, Eurykleia's best argument against Telemachos's voyage to Pylos is that his possessions at home need guarding:

And these men will devise evils against you, on your
      returning,
so you shall die by guile, and they divide all that is yours.
No, but stay here and guard your possessions.

(2.367–69)

We have already seen how the suitors have resorted to a strategy
of depleting Telemachos's inheritance in order to force (and "win")
Penelope's hand. The riches of every archaic dynasty, as any Trojan of
the time could have attested, were precarious enough. Those of the
House of Odysseus are especially vulnerable because Odysseus is not
at home to protect them. Thus, Telemachos is in jeopardy primarily
because he is fatherless.

The Homeric epics make it abundantly clear that a boy without a
father to protect him and his possessions would naturally be savagely
robbed of everything he has.[6] Take Andromache's famous speech to

Hector about the fate of their son, Astyanax, in which she points out that any boy without a father to protect him—even if he be the son of a hero and unthreatened by foreign enemies—will have his lands snatched away from him and be reduced to beggary.

> Though [Astyanax] escape the attack of the Achaians with all
>   its sorrows,
> yet all his days for your sake there will be hard work for him
> and sorrows, for others will take his lands away from him. The
>   day
> of bereavement leaves a child with no agemates to befriend
>   him.
> He bows his head before every man, his cheeks are bewept, he
> goes, needy, a boy among his father's companions,
> and tugs at this man by the mantle, that man by the tunic,
> and they pity him, and one gives him a tiny drink from a
>   goblet,
> enough to moisten his lips, not enough to moisten his palate.
> But one whose parents are living beats him out of the banquet
> hitting him with his fists and in words also abuses him:
> "Get out, you! Your father is not dining among us."
>   (*Il.*22.487–99)

In the *Odyssey*, the dangers to a boy whose father is dead or gone emerge explicitly several times. For example, in book 14, disguised as a Cretan, Odysseus recounts to Eumaios a plausible tale of his youth that treats the theme of the unprotected boy. The Cretan tells how he was born the illegitimate son of Kastor, a very prosperous man, and how Kastor nevertheless treated him as a legitimate son. When Kastor died, however, the other sons divided the inheritance among themselves. The Cretan claims that he survived this ordeal only because of his courage: "for I was no contemptible man, not one who fled from the fighting" (14.212–13).

Odysseus has great concern over what will happen to the estate that he left behind. In Hades, the first thing he asks his mother, Antikleia, is how she died. The second is about his lineage: "And tell me of my father and son whom I left behind. Is my inheritance still with them, or does some other man hold them now, and thinks I will come no more?" (11.174–76). This concern is especially important because

Telemachos is alone, a hard fact that Odysseus himself points up when he asks Telemachos in book 16 (before Odysseus reveals himself) why his son has not demanded the rights to his inheritance. Is it, Odysseus asks, because Telemachos cannot trust his own brothers to help him? Telemachos admits that he does not suffer from the treachery of brothers—because, in fact, he has none. He recounts how essentially lonely he is, and Homer reminds the audience that Odysseus's lineage is and always has been a very thin and delicate one. In each of the last three generations, there has been only one son born to carry on the name. Telemachos explains this in a very striking speech in which he uses the word *mounon* (lone) in a powerful triple anaphora, unparalleled in the rest of the *Odyssey*. Here is my own translation, which attempts to convey a sense of the Greek arrangement.

> So, the son of Kronos made ours a lonely line.
> One lone son, Laertes, was born to Arkesios,
> one lone son, Odysseus, to him; and Odysseus left
> one lone son in the halls, me, and got no good of it.
>
> (16.117–20)[7]

This chain of single-son generations and the consequent patrilineal fragility (especially since the grandfather is languishing and the father lost) goes a long way to explain Telemachos's diffidence. He knows that more is at risk in the situation on Ithaca than his life.[8]

This may explain the attention given to Laertes, despite his having no direct effect on the plot. Penelope's weaving of a shroud for Laertes takes on a new poetic and thematic beauty when we understand that it really is the fabric of the House of Odysseus that is in Penelope's hands. Laertes represents the House of Odysseus hanging on by a thread. Of course, Laertes will revive in book 23, and Athene will rejuvenate him when the three generations are united to defend the family.[9]

In *The Composition of Homer's "Odyssey,"* W. J. Woodhouse acknowledges that the welfare of the son is a constitutive theme in this epic. "Without Telemachos, no *Odyssey*," he writes (1930, 248). Woodhouse even goes so far as to claim,

> The simple but entirely adequate reason why Odysseus, and not some other of great personages of tradition, became the hero of

the Romance, lay in the fact that, among all the chieftains who survived the War, Odysseus alone had a son. (249)

Though Woodhouse's statement is not quite accurate, he rightly emphasizes the importance of the paternal line. Nestor could not have been the hero of the *Odyssey*, since he has several sons. Much less would have depended on his successful homecoming. However, it is more likely that what makes Odysseus worthy of the *Odyssey* is his attitude toward his son as he displays it in the *Iliad*.[10] The other Greek heroes at Troy boast that they are their fathers' sons. Odysseus—at two key moments when he wants to insist on what kind of man he really is—identifies himself as the father of his own son. When he reads the riot act to Thersites, he says,

> If once more I find you playing the fool, as you are now,
> nevermore let the head of Odysseus sit on his shoulders,
> let me nevermore be called Telemachos' father.
>
> > (*Il.* 2.258–60)

When Agamemnon questions his courage, Odysseus shoots back:

> How can you say that . . . I hang back from
> fighting? Only watch, if you care to and if it concerns you,
> the very father of Telemachos locked with the champion
> > Trojans,
> breaker of horses.
>
> > (*Il.* 4.351–55)

ODYSSEUS'S PARTING INJUNCTION

In book 18, in the presence of her son, the suitors, and the Cretan beggar, Penelope repeats the last words that Odysseus imparted to her as he embarked for Troy.

> "Dear wife, since I do not think the strong-greaved Achaians
> will all come safely home from Troy without hurt, seeing
> that people say the Trojans are men who can fight in battle,
> that they are throwers of the spear, and shooters of arrows,
> and riders with fast-footed horses, who with the greatest

speed settle the great and hateful issue of common battle,
I do not know if the god will spare me, of if I must be lost
there in Troy; here let everything be in your charge.
You must take thought for my father and mother here in our
    palace,
as you do now, or even more, since I shall be absent.
But when you see our son grown up and bearded, then you
    may
marry whatever man you please, forsaking your household.

                                   (*Od.* 18.259–70)

These dozen lines arguably form the most important passage for understanding Penelope's role in the plot of the *Odyssey*. Yet they pose particular problems; the issues are complex and have been made obscure in the extreme by criticism. R. D. Dawe has written in exasperation, "The variety of opinions expressed on this passage by Greek scholars of proven competence calls into question the reliability of any literary assessment of anything anywhere in Homer" (1993, 671).[11] Perhaps this is why some redactors have ignored the speech entirely. Samuel Butler skips any mention of it in the eighty-page retelling of the story that prefaces his *The Authoress of the "Odyssey,"* first published in 1897. More than a hundred years later in 2000, Stanley Lombardo does not include it in *The Essential Homer*.

Some scholars simply cannot square these words with their own notion of what an ideal warrior would say. Ulrich von Wilamowitz-Moellendorff is particularly strong in his disdain. To him, the whole notion that a hero as manly as Odysseus would ever have delivered such a cautious speech seemed utterly incredible and absurd. In *Heim-kehr*, Wilamowitz-Moellendorff writes:

> Whoever takes it seriously, steps into the same trap as the Suitors. Or would a hero, departing for war, talk about the fact that war is fatally dangerous? He would rather say, "wipe your tears, not every bullet hits home." (1927, 24)[12]

The last two lines of the parting speech provoke even greater confusion. For centuries, this has been extremely disturbing to the serious reader, and the problem of reconciling the text with the traditional view of who Penelope is and what Odysseus should want from her has led to the interpretive imbroglio noted by Dawe. Since Homer employs the imperative mood in these lines, Lattimore's translation ("But when you see our son grown up and bearded, then you may marry whatever man you please, forsaking your household,") is misleading. A better translation would be: "But as soon as you see your son with a beard, marry whomever you please and leave your house" (269–70). Thus, as Penelope reports it, Odysseus's injunction clearly means that she is *not* to marry before Telemachos has a beard but that she *must* remarry as soon as he gets one.

Most scholars attempt to solve the problem by assuming that Penelope is making the whole thing up. For example, John Winkler writes, "We might well suppose that Penelope's account of Odysseus' parting words about Telemakhos' beard is her own invention, on the spur of the moment" (1990, 147). E. Knox says flatly, "Penelope is lying when she reports Odysseus' injunction to her to marry" (*Ovid* 1995, 97). Ralph Hexter writes in *A Guide to the "Odyssey,"* "If this was what Odysseus had told her, he would indeed have felt the urgency to get back to Ithaka" (1993, 229).[13]

Surprisingly, in 1930, Woodhouse recognized the potential of the passage to make sense of the plot.

> Now it is obvious that the parting injunctions of Odysseus are decisive—if true. They explain everything, both the long years of delay in accepting marriage, and her present implied change of attitude. Nothing more was required than that she should quote those injunctions whenever the occasion demanded. (Woodhouse 1930, 86)

Nevertheless, concludes Woodhouse, the injunction is not true. Penelope has "just told a fib" (ibid.).

Joseph Russo attempts a slightly altered approach. He writes, "But it is not necessary to interpret this as a *lying* speech in order to see it as a speech intended to deceive and *mislead* the suitors" (1992, 66). Russo's idea is that though Penelope ends the speech with an admission that she must remarry, this speech actually will save her from having to do so.

The best justification for thinking that Penelope is deceiving the suitors is Odysseus's private response to what he thinks she is doing. Her words have moved the suitors to gape at her and then fetch gifts with the hope of impressing her. Odysseus, in disguise, watches all this, pleased by how his wife extracts wealth from suitors "while her own mind had other intentions" (*noos de hoi alla menoina*, 18.281–83). These "other intentions" are commonly taken to mean a plan to remain single. Fitzgerald's influential translation lays it out starkly:

> Odysseus's heart laughed when he heard all this—
> Her sweet tones charming gifts out of the suitors
> With talk of marriage, though she intended none.
>
> (18.281–83)

On the one hand, it is hard to imagine how Penelope could use Odysseus's parting injunction—fabricated or not—to further delay her remarriage. She, herself, claims Odysseus's words assure that "there will come that night when a hateful marriage is given to wretched me" (18.272–73), and Antinoös says flatly in his response to her words: "We [suitors] will not go back to our own estates, nor will we go elsewhere, until you marry whichever Achaian you fancy" (18.288–89). On the other hand, it is easy to imagine how the injunction might have served Penelope in the past when, by the very terms of the injunction, she was not supposed to consider remarriage. Years before the Odyssey opens, when Telemachos was still a boy, a firm public commitment to remarry as soon as her son was grown might have bought Penelope some time. In book 18, however, when Telemachos's age is no excuse, reminding the suitors of the injunction can only work against the preservation of her chastity. Unless Penelope is seriously preparing to remarry, she would not offer the suitors the added justification that they are promoting Odysseus's cause as well as their own.

As I see it, there would be only one way to use the injunction as a way to avoid remarriage. The terms of the injunction, as Penelope reports it, seem to stipulate that Odysseus be dead before Penelope remarries. Penelope might have insisted that there is no conclusive evidence that her husband is not still on his way home and enlist the support of the many guests and soothsayers who say that he is. She might then insist that the suitors have no legal right to court her. There is even evidence that such a defense could hold some sway with the suitors. When Agelaos tries to be reasonable to Telemachos in book 20, he says:

As long as the spirits in the hearts of you both were hopeful
that Odysseus of the many designs would have his
    homecoming,
then no one could blame you for waiting for him, and holding
the suitors off in the palace, since that was the better way for
    you
in case Odysseus did come home and return to his palace.

(20.328–32)

Nevertheless, Penelope repeatedly insists that Odysseus will not return. At her first appearance in book 1, she does not contradict her son
when he insists that there were many heroes besides Odysseus who lost
their homecoming day at Troy. Twice the suitors quote her as having
unequivocally stated that Odysseus is dead, and Penelope uses the
same words in reporting her own speech to the Cretan beggar: *epei
thane dios Odusseus* (since great Odysseus is dead 19.141 = 2.96 =
24.131). In book 4 Penelope confides to her maids in private, "for first
I lost a husband with the heart of a lion" (4.724), and a little later says
the same thing to the ghost of her sister Iphthime (4.814). Penelope is
unwavering. As late as book 23—speaking to Eurykleia, who has
shown that she would lay down her life rather than betray her lady—
Penelope says, "But Odysseus has lost his homecoming and lost his life,
far from Achaia" (23.67–68).

Unlike her son, Penelope willingly entertains soothsayers and itin-
erant guests who tell the news of Odysseus. Listening attentively,
Penelope indulges her grief and her longing and gives no intellectual
credence to the hopeful tales of return. Her invariable response to
prophecy is the equivalent of "if only it were so."

If only this word, stranger and guest, were brought to
    fulfillment,
soon you would be aware of my love and many gifts given
by me, so any man who met you would call you blessed.

(17.163–65 = 19.309–11)

Penelope uses the optative of wish to describe an alternate reality that
would be preferable but that is clearly out of the question. It is not ac-
tionable. Very similar is Penelope's use of the potential optative in her
response to Eurykleia in book 23.

Dear nurse, . . . You know
how welcome [Odysseus] would be if he appeared in the
    palace:
to all, but above all to me and the son we gave birth to.

(23.59–61)

Nothing that Penelope does to influence the plot is motivated by hope
that Odysseus will return. Quite the contrary, I would emphasize that
all of her actions and decisions are founded upon a conviction that
most likely her husband *is* dead and will not return. All her official and
confidential statements are to this effect; so that the traditional assumption that she has an expectation of Odysseus's return is our own
fantasy, either a product of our disdain for her ability to act or account
for herself, of an utter confusion of our own knowledge with hers, or of
our own sheer sentimentality.

Though we may *wish* her to do otherwise, the terms of the injunction enjoin Penelope to remarry when Telemachos has a beard, that is,
she is to assume that he is dead. This is what Penelope is patently
doing.

Since theories that Penelope is lying about the injunction or her
intention to follow it are untenable, we should be able to find logic in
Odysseus's parting words. Wilamowitz notwithstanding, Odysseus's
words to Penelope seem eminently sane and shrewd for a man departing to war, if that man's prime concern is to ensure the safety of his
oikos and keep it in the bloodline. Odysseus needed to make sure first
that his possessions were guarded assiduously until Telemachos could
do it for himself and, second, that Telemachos was never displaced by
another claimant to the estate. Imagine that Odysseus had been killed
in the fourth year of the war when Telemachos was still a small boy and
risked being treated as badly as Andromache knew her son would be.
By following the injunction, Penelope will not bring in a new husband
or bear a child that might challenge Telemachos's rights of inheritance.
A dozen years later, when Telemachos comes of age, Penelope will pro-
mote his claim to the *oikos* by allying herself (and her son) with the
strongest man possible and by moving to her new husband's *oikos*, giving Telemachos independence to manage his own. A prompt remarriage would have prevented the suitors from making common cause
and invading the house as they have done by the time the *Odyssey*
opens. The plan, of course, has gone awry. Even so, Penelope's remar-

riage can make all the difference. Though the suitors have made a pact to kill Telemachos and divide up the estate, would the chosen bridegroom really be eager to honor this deal? In book 22, Eurymachos betrays Antinoös as soon as he sees that Odysseus has the upper hand. Would the new husband slaughter the son of his new bride? Penelope's appearance before the suitors in book 18 may speak to this question. "Their knees gave way, and the hearts in them were bemused with passion, and each one prayed for the privilege of lying beside her" (18.212–13). Penelope's power to protect her son rests upon her ability to inspire loyalty in a new husband.

Still, one problem remains. If Penelope is intent upon following Odysseus's instructions, what is the reason that she is still at home? Why has she not remarried already? And why has she allowed the young lords to band together and present a united front against Telemachos? These are questions for the next chapter.

CHAPTER THREE

How Old Is Telemachos?

If the significant question of Telemachos's age in the *Odyssey* is whether or not he has gotten his beard, the answer must be that he certainly has, long ago. After all, he is twenty years old at least. If, however, the question is whether or not he has become a man, we have more to consider. Though a boy came into majority in classical Athens at fourteen years old and in Sparta at eighteen (Auffarth 1991, 425), we do not know at exactly what age the Homeric Greek youth was considered to be a man. The best measure we have is the age at which he got a beard (Auffarth 423). In Greek art, the bearded male is consistently a man, the unbearded one a boy. In the *Odyssey*, maturity (*nēbēs*) is explicitly linked twice to the new beard, once in regard to the form that Hermes takes to confront Odysseus (10.279) and again in the tale of the giant twins whom Apollo kills just in time. When they were only nine years old, the twins Otos and Ephialtes measured nine cubits wide and nine fathoms high and threatened to pile mountain upon mountain to climb the sky and attack the gods. The Olympians tolerated the boys only so long as they were not a real menace—that is, as long as they were without beards.

> Surely they would have carried it out if they had come to
>   maturity,
> but the son of Zeus whom Leto with ordered hair had borne
>   him,
> Apollo, killed them both, before ever the down gathered

below their temples, or on their chins the beards had
   blossomed.
$$(11.317-20)$$

Physically, Telemachos seems a rather mature twenty-year-old, a
fact that Athene carefully notes. "Big as you are" she says, in Lattimore's translation, or, as Fagels renders it, "You've sprung up so!"
(1.207). Later, Athene assures him: "You are big and splendid" (1.301).
A single month passes between this and book 21, where Telemachos
shows himself strong enough to string his father's bow, a feat that none
of the suitors who attempt it are able to achieve. In the meantime, he
ventures to the mainland, where he wins the admiration of several heroes. Later, he fights alongside his father in two battles. As with Otos
and Ephialtes, maturity is linked to the power to harm enemies and,
specifically, to extract revenge. Zeus holds that he warned Aigisthos
that Orestes would take vengeance as soon as he reached maturity and
hungered to reclaim what was his (1.41). Athene exhorts Telemachos
to be bold and to imitate Orestes. She urges him to consider "some
means by which you can force the suitors out of your household"
(1.270) and "by which you can kill [them] . . . by treachery or open attack" (1.295–96).[1] Telemachos is big enough and splendid enough,
physically, to accomplish it.

    There is another side to Telemachos. Before Athene visits Ithaca,
he is lost in daydreams and has no intention of taking action.

He sat among the suitors, his heart deep grieving within him,
imagining in his mind his great father, how he might come
   back
and all throughout the house might cause the suitors to
   scatter,
and hold his rightful place and be lord of his own possessions.
$$(1.114-17)$$

The full pathos of this scene emerges only when we remember that
Telemachos knows the futility of the dream he embraces. He openly
and thoroughly rejects the possibility that Odysseus will return home.

Easy for them, since without penalty they eat up the substance
of a man whose white bones lie out in the rain and fester

somewhere on the mainland, or roll in the wash of the
  breakers.
· · · · · · · · · ·
. . . as it is, he has died by an evil fate, and there is no comfort
left for us, not even though some one among mortals
tells us he will come back. His day of homecoming has
  perished.

(1.160–68)

Though Penelope is aware that Telemachos is a strapping young
man, she also knows that he is not ready to defend himself. She points
out that her son is still *nēpios* (childish) and incompetent to deal with
men in either battle or the assembly (4.818). In book 2, Telemachos
himself admitted the former characteristic and displayed the latter.
Athene would not debate the point. She is aware of this problem with
Telemachos and the very phrasing of her exhortation betrays it: "You
should not go on clinging to your childhood. You are no longer of an
age to do that" (1.296–97). Can Telemachos have reached the measure of manhood and be *nēpios* at the same time?

As obscure as the Greek notion of a child is, the notion of child-
ishness—behavior by adults more appropriate to children—is not.
This metaphorical sense of *nēpios* is applied to many characters in the
Iliad and the *Odyssey*, even (especially?) to Agamemnon. Cunliffe defines it variously as "feeble . . . childish, foolish, thoughtless, senseless,
credulous." Poor Telemachos, each of these senses can be—and has
been—used to explain his character. But I think none quite fit. Let us
look at them in turn.

TELEMACHOS'S CHARACTER

If it is true the Telemachos has more muscle than any of his enemies,
why does he not use it? Why has he neglected his father's weapons as
if he has never given a thought to a clash of arms? Why is he so certain that "soon [the suitors] will break me myself to pieces" (*Od.*
1.251)? Is his will feeble? Is he a coward? There is sufficient ready criticism from Athene in book 1 to make us wonder, not to mention the
much sharper reproof in book 16 by the disguised Odysseus, who insists
that even a lowly beggar such as himself would be ashamed to shrink
from battling the suitors.

If such things could be, another could strike my head from my
    shoulders
if I did not come as an evil thing to all those people
as I entered the palace of Odysseus, the son of Laertes.
And if I, fighting alone, were subdued by all their number,
then I would rather die, cut down in my own palace,
than have to go on watching forever these shameful activities.

                                (16.102–7)

Nevertheless, key details reveal that the beggar's taunt is not really
offered in good conscience. The beggar asks what is wrong: "Do you
find your brothers wanting? A man trusts help from these in the fighting when a great quarrel arises" (16.97–98). Of course, Telemachos's
problem is not that his brothers are weak or that he is afraid to rely on
them. He has no brothers, and the beggar knows it full well. "The son
of Kronos made ours a lonely line," Telemachos says, and (as I pointed
out in chapter 2) the repetition of *mounon* (lone) in the next three
verses hammers the point home. Telemachos is alone, but his enemies
seem "beyond numbering" (*murioi*). When he says for the second time,
"and soon [the suitors] will break me myself to pieces" (16.128),
Telemachos is not being cowardly, just accurate. Odysseus is well aware
of the odds. Can he possibly want his only son to make a suicidal as-
sault on the suitors? Such may be the way of Achilles, but it certainly
is not the way of the usually careful, always wily hero who prefers far
more to win by stealth than by bravado.[2] None of this evidence for
Telemachos's cowardice is compelling. If anything, Telemachos's decisions prove him to be quite levelheaded and prudent, and the pre-
ceding analysis, I think, ought to acquit him of foolishness as well.
Whether his departure for Pylos and Sparta is a foolish choice in itself
is a moot question: one would have to take that up with Athene.

Debate over whether Telemachos is *nēpios* has flourished in many
guises. Most striking are the varied opinions over the supposedly
thoughtless three lines with which, in book 1, he claims authority in
the house and dispatches his mother back to her quarters.[3] Stephanie
West thinks that it shows "callousness in this context." She argues,
"Certainly the favourable impression created by Telemachus' earlier
observations is quite destroyed by this adolescent rudeness . . ." (1988,
120). But is Telemachos really being cheeky? It is true that Penelope is
nonplused, but is that not because Telemachos has for the first time

found the pluck to make a claim to the responsibility that she has so long hoped he might shoulder? She takes his words seriously: "for she laid the serious words of her son deep away in her spirit" (*Od.* 1.361). There is no textual reason to think that she resents them.

As for senselessness, if Penelope finds her son lacking sense, neither Nestor nor Menelaos do. Even in book 2, so full of his callow attempts to assert himself, he shows eminently good sense and self-discipline by renouncing all political ambition in order to concentrate his efforts on minding his own house. Even the case for his credulousness is in some way quite weak. Like his mother—even more so, he says—he is not taken in by soothsayers. In book 2, he does not throw his lot in with Halitherses' prophesies. He even resists Helen's accommodating interpretation of the eagle and insistence that Odysseus "will come home and take revenge" or "is already home, and making a plan of evil for all of the suitors" (15.177–78).

> Then the thoughtful Telemachos said to her in answer:
> "May Zeus, high thundering husband of Hera, so appoint it.
> Then even at home I would make my prayers to you, as to a
>   goddess."
>
> (15.179–81)

What, then, is the matter with Telemachos? To answer this question, I believe that we should turn our attention to the epithet that Homer uses most often to describe him. At least forty-six times in the *Odyssey*, Telemachos is called *pepnumenos*. Of obscure derivation and uncertain meaning,[4] the word *pepnumenos* bears such translations as "thoughtful" (Lattimore), "wise" (Fitzgerald), "cautious" (Lawrence), "prudent" (Bates), "excellent person" (Butler), and "having good feeling" (Rouse). Cunliffe (1963) allows the definition "wise, of sound understanding, of good sense, astute, shrewd, sagacious." Hainsworth, in his commentary on book 8, recommends the translation "perfect gentleman." When applied to others, the epithet is clearly complimentary and indicates someone who speaks with honesty and frankness.[5] It is routinely connected to the heralds Medon and Peisenor, since honesty and frankness are the salient virtues of a herald.[6] When it is applied to Nestor and Menelaos, it is definitive. Athene assures Telemachos that Nestor "will not tell you any falsehood; he is too *pepnumenos*" (3.20). Nestor confidently asserts the same thing about Menelaos: "He will not tell you any falsehood; he is too *pepnumenos*" (3.328). The English translation that best captures the idea behind *pepnumenos*, I think, is "artless."

Artlessness pegs Telemachos's inability to be deceptive or to conceal his thoughts and feelings, and it poses the primary block to his maturation and his ability to assume leadership of the House of Odysseus. Telemachos is honest, frank, unguarded, naive—like a good child. His problem is that he is still clinging to this childhood—or, rather, has had no guidance for moving beyond it. Behavior that was a virtue in the boy is unsuitable now that he is a young man. Nor is it right for Telemachos to imitate Nestor or Menelaos. Successful old heroes like them can afford to be artless; a young man whose future is in the balance must confront the hostile and dishonest world on its own terms.

"Every culture and subculture teaches its young how to tell the truth—and how to deceive"—so Donald Lateiner writes in his *Sardonic Smile* (1995, 140). The Greeks are especially serious about the latter skill. Studying modern Greek culture, P. Walcot finds that "to lie does not constitute the moral crime which it has become in the sophisticated culture of Western Europe and North America" (1977, 7). Lying is not, however, "natural," even to the Greek peasants of Vasilika, the village that Walcot cites: "An inferior is vulnerable and must be taught to protect himself, and this process of education is not always pleasant" (19).

Of course, Telemachos's father could have taught Telemachos all he needed to know about deception. Odysseus is more than gifted at that art and employs it even when it may seem gratuitous and cruel. The best Greek antonym for *pepnumenos* could easily be one of Odysseus's epithets—for example, *polumētis*. Heroic honesty, the kind that is so dominant in the *Iliad*, plays almost no role in Odysseus's adventures. His cause is not advanced by it; his mind finds in it no charm. Odysseus may be fair to his companions, but he is rarely honest. He could have taught Telemachos well, if he had been around.

QUESTIONS OF BIRTH

If the son, therefore, is in jeopardy primarily because he has not had a father to protect him and to teach him what he needed to know to defend himself, the interesting question becomes what Telemachos thinks about Odysseus. When Athene, in book 1 of the *Odyssey*, darts down to Ithaca and stands at the palace gate disguised as Mentes, she pretends not to know the young man who welcomes her. A little later, she pretends to discern in him a resemblance to Odysseus and asks the young man whether her suspicions are true: is he actually the son of the great hero? Telemachos, who will withhold his father's name for almost another 150 lines, now attempts to put Athene's very question into question.

> See, I will accurately answer all that you ask me.
> My mother says indeed I am his. I for my part
> do not know. Nobody really knows his own father.[7]
>
> (1.214–16)

What can we make of Telemachos's philosophizing? What is being claimed, and who is claiming it?

For a long time, this passage was taken neither as a comment on Odysseus nor even as one primarily about Telemachos. Rather, it was read as if Homer were using it to reveal his own true opinion about women. Expecting to find moral teachings in Homer, seventeenth-century readers looked to blame someone for Telemachos's uncertainty. In the opinion of these moralists, if Telemachos could not be certain of his father, it was because he could not trust his mother. She may say that Odysseus is the father, but she may also be lying or merely too promiscuous to be certain herself. This *cherchez la femme* mentality is what Madame Dacier had to contend with in the notes to her 1731 translation of the *Odyssey*. In her note to *Odyssey* 1.214–16, she writes, "Here is a passage that has been much misused against women, as if Telemachos had sought to mock them, which is false."[8] Unable to believe that Telemachos intends to impugn Penelope's virtue as if he "wanted to doubt and to make doubtful her wisdom and loyalty,"[9] Dacier proceeds to offer something like the modern interpretation of *Odyssey* 1.216, arguing, in effect, that the male's uncertainty about the genuineness of his offspring occurs not because he is the dupe of woman but because he is victim of the natural logic of maleness. Only woman gives birth; only she has direct evidence that the child is of her flesh. The bond between father and son is naturally putative. She cites Euripides as evidence. She then uses Menander to go further and claim that no one knows his own father: one has only suspicions and faith.

This ontological argument might be pushed a step further. If a man cannot be as certain about his biological link to the child as a woman can about hers, the child has even less certainty about its link to either parent. As Fitzgerald translates *Odyssey* 1.216, "Who has known his own engendering?" The child, though present at the birth, cannot remember it. Any child is therefore as intellectually uncertain of its mother as of its father. This fact is not overlooked by Homer or Telemachos. The Greek word that Lattimore translates as "father" is not *patera* but *gonon* (parentage). Expanded in this way, Telemachos's question either rises to philosophy or sinks to cliché. West argues, "the idea must already have been commonplace, and the tone is surely mildly ironical, though Telemachos might well be somewhat diffident in asserting that the hero whom his visitor knows so much better and so much admires is in fact his father (1988, 102–3). I do not see any diffidence here. I see a repudiation. In the next two lines, Telemachos tells exactly the sort of father that he would rather have had: "But how I wish I could have been rather son to some fortunate man, whom old age overtook among his possessions." (*Od.* 1.217–18). Telemachos is telling just what he feels.

How else should he feel? Some rage from an adolescent toward an absent father is certainly not surprising or unreasonable. What Telemachos has inherited from his father is a threatened and threatening identity. Arthur Adkins writes:

> Telemachus . . . is despondent, thinking not of his [*aretē*], but of his generally wretched condition. People say he is the son of Odysseus, the [*apotmotatos*] of mankind, but he for his part does not know whether it is true. In either case, in his present state of dejection, he does not feel that it would affect his [*aretē*] much; for he is not at the moment conscious of himself as [*agathos*]. (1972, 18)

Why should Telemachos want to admit to being the son of a man he has never seen, when it is likely to do nothing but destroy his life? Still, there is a genuine philosophical side to the problem. While until quite recently, no one could have any certainty about his or her genetics, it is also true that one usually had to act as though one had. In Telemachos's case, the indeterminacy of his parentage is emblematic of his indeterminate future. He is being squeezed into a corner with little or no hope of success. He will lose his life, his estate, or both, which is enough to make anyone despondent.

As Telemachos wrestles with his questions, Penelope is attempting to determine if his answers reveal him to be ready to defend himself against his enemies. The import of this passage transcends Telemachos's mind alone and introduces a question thematic to the *Odyssey* as a whole: how does one live and act in the face of partial knowledge?

PAIDEUSIS

The question of Telemachos's maturity has occupied commentators on the *Odyssey* almost as much as it occupies Penelope within the epic. It is generally recognized that Telemachos is not yet a man at the outset of the epic and that he there acts out of what Lydia Allione calls *"sua passiva fanciulezza"* (1963, 16). But there is no general agreement on whether or when Odysseus's son matures. Essentially, all the critics take one of three points of view: either he does not change at all, he is transformed all at once by Athene, or he goes through a slow maturation on his journey to Pylos and Sparta.

The first view is most notably represented by Wilamowitz-Moellendorff, who categorically rejected that character development (*Charakterentwickelung*) is possible in Greek literature.[10] Yet despite Wilamowitz-Moellendorff's authority and the protection he can provide against the abuses of Neoplatonic or Jungian interpretations of the Telemachy, few people nowadays can accept that Telemachos does not change at all. Allione championed the simple, all-at-once approach to Telemachos's change, which emphasizes Athene's power to catalyze the transformation.[11]

Most scholars embrace a third approach, the so-called *paideusis* (education), which allows for Telemachos to develop gradually. Agathe Thornton, for example, begins her chapter on Telemachos unequivocally: "It is well known that in the course of the *Odyssey* Telemachus grows from boyhood to manhood" (1970, 68). Hölscher has attempted to effect a compromise between the second and the third approach. Though he believes that "the one change is change enough," Hölscher asserts that Telemachos's first step toward maturity must be fleshed out by later experiences. "The entire *Telemachy*," he writes, "is nothing other than the transformation of the folktale formulation, 'when our son has grown a beard,' into various epic situations" (1996, 139). Opinions vary, of course, about the nature and the pace of the developmental change and about its turning point, if any. Clarke, for example, writes: "For Telemachus, [being accepted into Nestor's household] has been a tonic experience after the desperation of his life at Ithaca, and at last he is ready to break out of the shell of his depression and uncertainty and make his way in broad heroic society" (1969, 32).

Norman Austin deserves credit for perceiving in his 1969 article "Telemachos Polymechanos" that the *paideusis* is the change of an initially "candid and ingenuous young man" (1969, 52)[12] into one who knows how to use deception. For him, however, it is Athene, not Odysseus, who serves as instructor: "Athena proceeds to educate Telemachos into consciousness of himself as the son of Odysseus and of the responsibility which that entails by the Socratic method" (52).[13] Austin's Telemachos is a quick study indeed. Austin notes that by the end of book 1, Telemachos has shown himself "an apt pupil in Athena's school," already lying like the master.

> More precisely, [Telemachos] tells not one but three lies in quick succession (1.413–419): "My father will never return," he says. "I no longer am swayed by messengers who may chance by or by the pronouncements of seers whom my mother may invite in. The stranger you ask about was Mentes, an old friend of my father's." The last lie is of Athena's making, second-hand material lying conveniently to hand for the occasion. But the first two, which spring from Telemachos's own quick intelligence, show him as much capable of personal initiative in mendacity as in other activities of life. Now, as never before, Telemachos has reason to think his father alive and to respect the words of messengers or seers. It is the suitors who cannot recognize a messenger and mock at prophecies. (54)[14]

Telemachos's supposed skill at deceit poses no wonder for Austin, who finds that Telemachos has it bred in the bone.

> It would be a strange thing indeed if, with Autolykus for great-grandfather, Odysseus for father, Penelope for mother and Athena for divine patron, Telemachus should grow to manhood with not a trace of the congenital proclivity for deception, or if we prefer, for artful invention. (46)

For Austin, Telemachos's *paideusis* is a question not really of education but, rather, of Athene's reminding Telemachos whose son he is.

The *paideusis* cannot be denied. Telemachos begins the *Odyssey* as an ineffectual, if not wholly passive, character, at a loss how to defend himself. Athene points out more than once that there are two ways to attack the suitors, openly or by stealth (*ēe dolōi ē ampadon*, *Od.* 1.296). For the young man without allies, open attack against an overwhelming number of suitors was out of the question. Stealth, for the artless boy, was equally impossible. Yet by the end of the epic, Telemachos has learned both tactics. Telemachos takes his heroic place next to his father and grandfather in battle against the Ithacan populace. Telemachos becomes a self-assured man, and the House of Odysseus enjoys renewed vigor: "You will see, dear father, if you wish, that as far as my will goes, I will not shame my blood that comes from you, which you speak of" (24.511–12). The grandfather is filled with pride. "What day is this for me, dear gods? I am very happy. My son and my son's son are contending over their courage" (24.514–15).

When are we to understand the principal turning point in Telemachos's maturation to be? Does it occur before the *Odyssey* opens, in Telemachos's recognition that the suitors are robbing him, or in book 1, when he asserts his rights? Is it grounded in Telemachos's experience of Athene, his decision to travel, his embrace of courtly life at Sparta, his decision to return home, his recognition of his father, the assertions of hospitality that he gives in the beggar's favor, his near drawing of the bow? In fact, though Telemachos's struggle is central to the story, the plot requires that Telemachos not be an effective agent until quite late in it.[15] Furthermore, from a narratological point of view, the dramatic pressure placed on Penelope would be prematurely released if Telemachos prematurely matured.

The problem with most interpretations of the *paideusis* is that they tend to rush Telemachos's progress and ignore the significance of what does not quickly change. Consequently, they tend to undo the dramatic tension that fuels the Ithaca-centered plot. The ineluctable truth is that upon his return to Ithaca, Telemachos is, if anything, less prepared and much less willing than he ever has been to fight for his rights.

For the turning point in Telemachos's maturation, we must seek a confluence of maturity and agency and an appropriate time that does not falsify the epic's dramatic structure. Thus, Telemachos's story ought to conform to four guidelines: Telemachos's maturation ought to be a consequence of his reunion with Odysseus, it ought to employ a major deception, it ought to be a moment of crisis that only Telemachos can resolve, and it ought to come late enough not to make Penelope's decision moot. Therefore, I propose an analysis of the plot that keeps the question of Telemachos's maturity open until the twenty-first book. Telemachos shows progress before that, but I think that he truly comes into his own only during the contest of the bow.[16]

THE PACE OF MATURATION

The morning before Penelope announces the contest, the suitors resolve to assassinate Telemachos immediately. The plan is stalled, however, by the fortuitous flight of a bird that persuades the suitors to postpone their plot (a decision they promptly regret)[17] in order to enjoy the pleasures of the feast that is being laid out for a festival in honor of Apollo. By the time Penelope announces the contest and the twelve axes are arranged in the great hall, the suitors must be quite drunk. Drunkenness no doubt underlies their inability to string the bow and Antinoös's postponement of the competition until the morrow, when he and the others will be better prepared for the challenge. The axes are left in place. Then, with "crafty intention" (*dolophroneōn, Od.* 21.274), resourceful Odysseus asks for a try at the bow. Penelope is willing to permit his attempt, although she makes clear that there is no question of his taking the prize. To prove it, she retires.[18]

Once Penelope is gone, Eumaios grabs the bow in an attempt to deliver it into Odysseus's hands, until the suitors, en masse, raise a hue and cry against Eumaios and threaten to kill him if he persists. Intimidated, Eumaios puts the bow down, thereby placing Odysseus's entire plan in jeopardy. At this point, Telemachos finally takes the initiative. He harshly commands Eumaios to deliver the bow and adds his own threats of violence. The manner in which he does this is of the greatest import. Telemachos pretends to vent his anger for the suitors on old Eumaios.

> Take care, or, younger though I am, I might chase you
> out to the fields with a shower of stones. I am stronger than
> you are.
> I only wish I were as much stronger, and more of a fighter
> with my hands, than all these suitors who are here in my
> household.

So I could hatefully speed any man of them on his journey out
    of our house,
where they are contriving evils against us.

                             (21.370–75)

Telemachos's tacit admission of physical inferiority to the suitors is also a sign that he has lowered his moral standards to theirs. Earlier in book 17, Telemachos had taken the high moral ground, defending Eumaios against Antinoös, saying, "Antinoös is nasty like that—provoking people with harsh words and egging them on" (17.394–95, Lombardo's translation). Now, Telemachos disperses all fears that he is acting seriously, righteously, or even nobly. Parading a seemingly artless animosity toward his enemies before their very eyes, Telemachos also persuades the suitors that he has nothing up his sleeve. He succeeds in pretending that he is not able to pretend. Thus, though the suitors had felt a threat of danger when Telemachos departed for Pylos, he now assures them that he is still the harmless child or even the fool.

The trick works. "So he spoke, and all the suitors laughed happily at him, and all gave over their bitter rage against Telemachos" (21.376–77). Homer's solution to the problem of Telemachos's maturation is therefore brilliant. In one stroke, without relieving the intense pressure on Penelope to decide how to act, he proves Telemachos to be a man, a worthy son to his wily father, and an active, effective, and decisive agent in the plot. And the bow arrives safely into Odysseus's hands.

CHAPTER FOUR

Penelope as Tragic Heroine

In book 16 of the *Odyssey*, Penelope learns of the second plot against her son's life—or, rather, of the persistence of the first. It is evident to her that only an immediate remarriage holds any hope of saving him.[1] Later the next day, she will confess her intention to the Cretan.

> Now I cannot escape from this marriage; I can no longer
> think of another plan; my parents are urgent with me
> to marry; my son is vexed as they eat away our livelihood;
> he sees it all; he is a grown man now, most able
> to care for the house, and it is to him Zeus grants this
>   [happiness in possessions].
>
> (19.157–61)

The night that transpires between the end of book 16 and the beginning of book 17 must have been a horrible one for Penelope, as she no doubt wrestled with conflicting feelings about remarriage. This is the night of her disturbing dream of the twenty geese. Later in this chapter, I will look closely at that dream. Right now, I will do no more than note that Penelope's distress over the dream seems to be the reason that she commands Eumaios to fetch the Cretan vagabond, the mysterious guest who "seems like a man who has wandered widely" (17.511).

THE THREAT OF BEGUILEMENT

In book 1, when Penelope hears of the new guest in the house, she asks Eumaios to fetch him so that she may learn what he knows about Odysseus. Apparently, such a request is not unusual. Penelope habitually entertains travelers, and they routinely spin wild tales about Odysseus, which moves Penelope to mournful tears, something that Eumaios accepts as "the right way for a wife when her husband is far and perished" (14.130). If there is sometimes danger in these tales—and Eumaios admits that he was once made a fool of by an Aitolian man who persuaded him of Odysseus's imminent return (14.378–85)—usually, there is none for Penelope. "Old sir," Eumaios had told the Cretan, "there is none who could come here, bringing a report of him, and persuade his wife and his dear son" (14.122–23). In fact, early in book 14—before the stranger shows what he can do—Eumaios advises him to earn handsome gifts at the palace by regaling Penelope with whatever skillful fantasy about Odysseus's return he could.

What is probably unusual about Penelope's request on this occasion is that she is forced to make it three times. Eumaios seems particularly worried about the Cretan's powers and consequently reluctant to fetch the man. Once Eumaios has heard this stranger's art, he realizes that this man is no amateur fabulist. Though he warned the man not to attempt to beguile him with lies (14.386–87), Eumaios admits to Penelope that that is just what the stranger did for three whole nights (17.515–21). These tales, he tells Penelope, would beguile her as well (17.514).

The word that Eumaios uses to describe the Cretan's power is *thelgein*. Between the *Iliad* and the *Odyssey*, there is a telling change in the meaning of this Greek verb, nicely revealed by Lattimore in his use of "maze" to translate it in the one and "beguile" (usually) to render it in the other. In the *Iliad*, immortals maze mortals, usually by employing their superior force. Zeus strikes with his thunderbolt; Hermes mazes with his staff. It is the eyes that are affected. The victim is forcibly blocked, diverted, or pushed aside from the object of desire. The hero strives to kill one man, but, instead, another gets in his way, or the hero finds himself chopping vainly at thin air. The hero suffers great frustration because his will remains untouched by the charm. In contrast, *thelgein* in the *Odyssey* is affected through the ears. It comes by way of words and alters the will itself.[2] Lured into an alternate course, the victim forgets the original goal and is transformed into a collabo-rator in his or her own destruction. The victim is pulled, not pushed; seduced, not thwarted. The fundamental mechanism is the seductive song of the Sirens.

> You will come first of all to the Sirens, who beguile [*thelgousin*][3]
> of all mankind and whoever comes their way; and that man
> who unsuspecting approaches them, and listens to the Sirens
> singing, has no prospect of coming home and delighting
> his wife and little children as they stand about him in
> greeting,
> but the Sirens by the melody of their singing beguile
> [*thelgousin*] him.
>
> (12.39–44)

Odysseus is no match for these weird creatures, who destroy without lifting a finger. He begs to be allowed to pursue the overwhelming de-sire that the Sirens kindle in him. Absent the will of his men rowing onward, wax in their ears, strapping him ever tighter to the mast, Odysseus would have tossed his life away on those rocks.

In the *Odyssey*, to beguile is also what a bard does, employing words to entice the ears. The audience listens, and "they are impas-sioned and strain to hear it when he sings to them" (17.520). To em-brace the well-made tale is a virtuous pleasure for the Homeric man or woman, but an excess of it must also be guarded against. Getting too involved exposes one to being deceived and cheated, as Eumaios was by the Aitolian. One must be careful not to confuse fiction with reality, truth with the pleasing lie. One must remain *apistos*, that is, skeptical, suspicious, mistrustful.[4]

Eurykleia tells her, "your heart was always mistrustful (*apistos*)" (23.72). But is Penelope sufficiently wary to resist the beguilements of this formidable master of his art, the Cretan beggar? Eumaios's lack of response to Penelope's second command to fetch the stranger seems to indicate that he is not sure. Nevertheless, some twenty lines later, Eu-maios does obey a third request without protest. It seems that Penelope finds a way in the space of those lines to instill confidence in the faith-ful old servant that she will be able to listen to the stranger's stories without forgetting that they are mere fictions.

Penelope has just made a bitter complaint about the suitors, voicing a wish that they disappear and insisting that her wish would have teeth if Odysseus could return. He would surely kill them all. Suddenly, Telemachos breaks forth in a loud sneeze that resounds through the halls, and Penelope, laughing, addresses Eumaios:

> "Go, please, and summon the stranger into my presence. Do you not see how my son sneezed for everything I have spoken? May it mean that death, accomplished in full, befall the suitors each and all, not one avoiding death and destruction."
>
> (17.544–47)

Though the evidence that sneezes were considered to be omens comes from much later antiquity (see Russo 1992, 44), this incident only makes sense if Penelope is responding to some actual superstition. Still, it is not at all obvious to me that Penelope is taking that superstition seriously, despite the fact that all interpreters of this passage that I know of have assumed that she does. It seems unlikely that Penelope, who has accepted no signs or reports of Odysseus's return and who will continue to reject them after this, should glibly accept this sneeze as a sure omen. Instead, I would argue that this is one time that we ought to consider not taking Penelope at her word. My method throughout this book has been to insist that Penelope's accounts of her own thoughts and motivations be accepted whenever there is no clear textual evidence to indicate that we should not. Here, in Penelope's first laugh, we can have this evidence. This is the first time that Penelope laughs, and laughter is quite uncharacteristic of her. It can only be a moment of lighthearted pretense that mocks the sort of mind that naively accepts the wish as substitution for the reality. Eumaios gets the message, as should we.[5]

When Penelope finally meets the Cretan, she is gracious and attentive, though at first the Cretan refuses to talk about himself. At length, however, feigning reluctance, the beggar tells his story, which is a tissue of lies, a colossal fabrication, and worthy of the Cretan birth that he claims. Whether or not Callimachus's opinion (*Hymn* 1.8) that all Cretans are liars was proverbial in Homer's time, the Homeric audience probably knew that Minos, the great king of Crete whom the beggar claims as his grandfather, was the constructor of the labyrinth. It was impossible for those who wandered into the labyrinth to find their way out. So, a Cretan is a master deceiver. This particular Cretan seems especially adept at fashioning his lies to satisfy his audience, adding new twists to his web of deceit to entangle Penelope better. For example, when he tells the tale to Eumaios, he makes himself out to be the bastard son of a rich Cretan; in his tale to Penelope, he is of pure noble stock. It is a good tale told well: "He knew how to say many false things that were like true sayings" (*Od.* 19.203).

Moved profoundly, Penelope immerses herself in her memories and her grief. Then follows one of literature's most beautiful similes: her cheeks stream with tears like a mountain flooded with snowmelt in the spring. Even so, Penelope's response is more or less independent of whether she believes that the Cretan is telling the truth. After she takes "her pleasure of tearful lamentation," she asks the Cretan to verify his story.

> Now, my friend, I think I will give you a test, to see if
> it is true that there, and with his godlike companions,
> you entertained my husband, as you say you did, in your
>   palace.
>
> (19.215–17)

In a very cagey manner, pretending not to know the significance of what he knows, the Cretan describes the clothes that Odysseus wore at the time. This proves to Penelope that the Cretan had seen Odysseus twenty years ago, and she says so. However, it does not mean that Odysseus will return home, and she says this, too (19.257–60). The Cretan protests. In doing so, he uses truth: "For I say to you without deception, without concealment, that I have heard of the present homecoming of Odysseus." But he also uses lies: "He is near, in the rich land of the men of Thesprotia" (19.269–71). He then offers to swear a firm oath that what he has predicted will happen. "Some time within this very year Odysseus will be here, either at the waning of the moon or at its onset" (306–7). Penelope is no more impressed by this solemn oath than Eumaios was by the one the Cretan gave to him in book 14. As emotional as she is, she remains *apistos*. Penelope says categorically: "But here is the way I think in my mind, and the way it will happen. Odysseus will never come home again" (19.312–13).

THE STRUGGLE TURNS INWARD

At this point, the Cretan goes off to have his feet washed by Eurykleia, who recognizes Odysseus's scar when she sees it. During the very long digression in which the poet relates the exciting story of how the young Odysseus was gored by a wild boar, Penelope is left sitting wordlessly apart by the fire, absorbed in her own meditation. When the Cretan finally returns to the fire, she begins the conversation: "Friend, I will stay here and talk to you, just for a little" (*Od.* 19.509). R. D. Dawe translates this line, "Stranger, there is still one little thing I will myself ask you," and then adds a very catty commentary.

> Words which would sound more natural if we were in a continuously flowing conversation. But in our texts Penelope's last words were some one hundred and fifty lines ago, and her little question now is itself to be delayed by some adventitious moralizing and mythology. When we finally hear it (535), we find it to be one of extraordinary silliness. (1993, 715)

Dawe is right in one respect. The words do sound like a continuation, which, from Penelope's point of view, they undoubtedly are. Emerging from her brown study, Penelope decides to reveal in full detail what is weighing on her mind, and it is strikingly consistent with her last thoughts before the Cretan went to get washed. Therefore, whereas Dawe dismisses this line with a decided upturn of his nose, as a petty addition to the conversation, I take it to be the heart of the poem's plot and message.

Penelope now takes the Cretan completely into her confidence, revealing the extremity of the mental pain that she suffers. There are two distinct kinds of pain. One dominates the day; the other haunts the night. By day, Penelope suffers grief over thoughts of her husband. This is a manageable sorrow, she says (*kērdomenon per, Od.* 511)—one that allows her enough peace of mind to tend to her household duties and supervise her maids. There is even a certain joy in her grief (*terpom' oduromenē*, 513), as if it rewarded her with some hidden, but vital, energy. This daytime sorrow is of a kind with the woes of other people, and one can usually find some escape from it in the sweet rest (*hēdeos hōrē*, 510) of delicious sleep (*hupnos glukeros*, 511). If Penelope can find no such rest, it is because she is tortured at night by an altogether different and uncompromising sort of pain, a measureless anguish (*penthos ame-trēton*, 512) without the least hint of joy: "Sharp anxieties . . . torment my sorrowing self" (19.516–18). These anxieties emerge from a bitter dilemma that she has not been able to resolve: "So my mind is divided and starts one way, then another" (19.524).

Penelope describes with great precision both horns of her dilemma. As she explains it in the next verses, her choice is between staying at home and leaving.

> Shall I stay here by my son and keep all in order,
> my property, my serving maids, and my great high-roofed
>   house,
> keep faith with my husband's bed and regard the voice of the
>   people,
> or go away at last with the best of all those Achaians
> who court me here in the palace with endless gifts to win me?
>   (19.525–29)

Penelope knows, as it should be clear to us now, that if she wants to save her son and preserve the House of Odysseus, her best course of action is to remarry and leave. But the other course tempts her and is the source of a nighttime anguish that implies a connection between her own story and the cause of the nightingale's pain.

> As when Pandareos' daughter, the greenwood nightingale,
> perching in the deep of the forest foliage sings out
> her lovely song, when springtime has just begun; she, varying
> the manifold strains of her voice, pours out the melody,
>   mourning
> Itylos, son of the lord Zethos, her own beloved
> child, whom she once killed with the bronze when the
>   madness was on her;
> so my mind is divided and starts one way, then another.
>   (19.518–24)

Unlike Itylos, Telemachos is not yet dead. Penelope's agony apparently stems from a fear that she could be a threat to his well-being. For understanding Penelope's psychology it would be helpful to be able to discern whether the allusion implies any malice on Penelope's part toward

Telemachos. Unfortunately, from Homer's brief account alone, it is not clear whether the crime against Itylos was committed willingly or not.

The key phrase *di'aphradias*, translated by Lattimore as "when the madness was on her," may indicate intentionality or be proof against it. There are precedents in the *Odyssey* for both. In book 14, for instance, the phrase is used for the soldier at Troy who "carelessly" has neglected to take his cloak along on an all-night watch. This could hardly be intentional. In book 17, it is used to describe Melanthios's intentional attempt to kick Odysseus out of the road. Trying to decide the issue, scholars have looked to two later versions of the story—one found in the scholia and one found among the Attic authors—which are unfortunately quite different from each other.[6] In the scholia, the nightingale is named Aëdon. Because she envies Niobe's large family, Aëdon attempts to kill Niobe's eldest son but, confused by the darkness of the night, mistakenly kills her own son instead. The Attic version tells the tale of Procne, a woman enraged at her husband for his adultery. To exact revenge, Procne deliberately kills their son and serves him to her husband for dinner. W. W. Merry prefers the former version in his commentary and so would render the crucial *di'aphradias* as "unwittingly," while Russo favors "in her senseless folly" because he accepts the latter interpretation.[7] I prefer to emphasize what the two versions have in common—namely, that the grievous act resulted from a mother's passion for something other than her son. Aëdon lets her envy control her; Procne, her jealousy. So, what is the threat to Telemachos? What is tempting Penelope to remain at home?

In the first place, remarriage means a break with all she knows and loves. Penelope loves the house where she has spent her best years, and she loves Odysseus. In a new home, she might reasonably be expected to curb her grief over the loss of her old life. More important, I think, remarriage would also mean the loss of her reputation and personal glory, her *kleos*, which depends on what the majority of Ithacans say about her. The Ithacans seem to hold the cynical view that most women in Penelope's situation would act selfishly, choosing the best of the Achaians and going away with him to enjoy the comfort and wealth that he could provide. Like the great misogynist Agamemnon, they seem to assume that sexual fidelity among women is a rare virtue indeed. Penelope, however, has held their respect until now because she has not remarried. Remarriage would compromise her *kleos*. I will return to this theme at the end of this chapter.

THE DREAM OF THE TWENTY GEESE

Penelope asks the Cretan to listen to and interpret a dream that she had the previous night that disturbed her greatly: "But come, listen to a dream of mine and interpret it for me" (*Od.* 19.535). A proper interpretation, she suspects, holds the key to healing the split in her mind.

Among Homeric dreams, the dream in book 19 of the *Odyssey* is unique in at least one respect. "Of several dreams in Homer, only this one," writes Russo, "resembles a true dream: its message is hidden in a symbolic code" (1992, 102). Dodds concurs, "This is the only dream in Homer which is interpreted symbolically" (1951, 106). The central symbol is the gaggle of twenty geese that begins and ends the dream. These geese also link the dream to the waking world in a kind of imitation of the meaning of the dream itself. It is hard to tell exactly at which point in the first two lines the dream begins. The last three lines as well tend to blur the boundary between dream and waking reality. Penelope's search for the geese after she awakens assures us that these are actually household pets that are close at hand.

> I have twenty geese here about the house, and they feed on
> grains of wheat from the water trough. I love to watch them.
> . . . .
> So he spoke; and then the honey-sweet sleep released me,
> and I looked about and saw the geese in my palace, feeding
> on their grains of wheat from the water trough, just as they
>   had been.
>
> (Od. 19.536–53)

One way to approach the analysis of the dream of the twenty geese is to see it as a core dream that gets three distinct interpretations in the *Odyssey*. The dream interprets itself, the Cretan evaluates the dream, and Penelope makes her final judgment about its meaning.

The Core Dream

In Penelope's dream of the twenty geese, an eagle swoops out of the sky, slaughters all of the geese, and swerves back to its mountain. Penelope is left in bitter sorrow at the loss.

But a great eagle with crooked beak came down from the
    mountain,
and broke the necks of them all and killed them. So the whole
    twenty
lay dead about the house, but he soared high in the bright air.
Then I began to weep—that was in my dream—and cried out
aloud, and around me gathered the fair-haired Achaian
    women
as I cried out sorrowing for my geese killed by the eagle.
(Od. 19.538–43)

The focus of this passage is on the intensity of the sorrow (*oiktr' olo-phuromenēn*) that Penelope feels in the dream itself (*en per oneirōi*). Why should Penelope have to remind her listener that she is describing a dream? How are we to take the "*per*" in line 541? The particle can be read as either an intensifier or a sign of opposition—in English, as either "even" or "even though." Penelope could be using it to distance herself from the actual importance of the emotion, as in Fagel's translation ("only a dream, of course"), or as a way of revealing its exceptional intensity, as is hinted at in Rieu's translation ("though it was only a dream").[8] However, since there can be little doubt, I think, that Penelope would feel sorrow in waking life if the pets that she loves were slaughtered, the particle only makes sense if the assumption is, rather, that she might not be as prone to weep over them in a dream as she would be in waking life.[9] The *per*, then, emphasizes her extreme attachment to the geese and her awareness that dreams are not reality but may well feel like it. Thus, the core of the dream seems to be the product of a high anxiety whose waking source is whatever the geese symbolize.[10]

The Eagle Interprets

The eagle of the dream returns and offers a symbolic interpretation of the geese.

But [the eagle] came back again and perched on the jut of the
gabled roof. He now had a human voice and spoke aloud to me:
"Do not fear, O daughter of far-famed Ikarios.
This is no dream, but a blessing real as day. You will see it
done. The geese are the suitors, and I, the eagle, have been

72

a bird of portent, but now I am your own husband, come
   home,
and I shall inflict shameless destruction on all the suitors."

(Od. 19.544–50)

The dream seems to pull out all the stops in endorsing its own interpretation. Returning with a compassionate human voice and a com-
forting message, the eagle insists that this is no dream (*onar*) but a
"blessing real as day," an auspicious and expected waking reality
(*hupar*). Essentially, his is a claim to objective truth. In other words,
the eagle wants to assure Penelope that what he is about to say has
more authority than a mere dream: *hupar* is more dependable than
onar. As if this were not enough, he also claims authoritative truth: he
is no less a reliable source than Odysseus himself, Penelope's own dear
husband. We can compare this claim to Agamemnon's dream in *Iliad*
2, where Zeus has employed the strategy of making the dream more authoritative by casting the dream messenger in the form of the wise and
artless Nestor.

The eagle's message is that the dream is not what it seems. Whatever Penelope may think, the dream is not actually a sad one, since
those who are slaughtered are not her pet geese but only the suitors,
whom the geese merely symbolize. That her dream tears are dried
seems to indicate that Penelope accepts the eagle's interpretation.
Most critics accept it at face value. Rutherford comments, "This dream
explains itself: the geese are the suitors, the eagle Odysseus" (1992,
194). The dream is taken, then, as a kind of prophesy. In fact, Lattimore amplifies his translation with that notion by rendering the
Greek—translated literally, "but I who was formerly the eagle bird"—
with the phrase "and I, the eagle, have been a bird of portent"
(19.548–49). A common assumption is that Homer is doing more than
merely teasing his audience; he is trying once again to tip Penelope off
to his plans for Odysseus.

Accepting the reliability of the eagle's interpretation has inevitably
led to psychoanalytic investigation of Penelope's unconscious thoughts.
George Devereux, for instance, who rather petulantly dismisses "the
psychological scotomata of philologists to complex psychological over-
tones in great literary works," (1957, 385) applies a psychoanalytic
method to prove that "Penelope cried over her geese for the simple reason that unconsciously she enjoyed being courted" (382). Devereux's

73

conclusion is picked up and amplified by Anne Rankin, who believes that "in the dream, and this is the crux of the matter, these emotions are for the suitors!" (1962, 620; the exclamation point seems appropriate). The Devereux-Rankin analysis approximates walking on stilts: it affords a way of looking down on things but is awkward and precarious. For it to work, Penelope would have to have identified the geese with the suitors beforehand, at least in her unconscious mind. Rankin insists that Penelope has equated the two.

> As the elucidation of the symbolism of the eagle and the geese takes place within the dream, we can assume Penelope's awareness from its beginning of the equation of geese with suitors and eagle with Odysseus. (1962, 619–20)

Rankin is here assuming that the eagle's interpretation is objectively correct and definitive. But the eagle and his interpretation are part of the dream. As such, they are part of its strategy. Of course, the analysis of any dream can become as endless and circular as a Möbius strip, like the well-known conundrum of the man who dreams that he is a butterfly but cannot be sure that he is not really a butterfly dreaming that he is a man. But why is the dreaming Penelope comforted by the eagle's insistence that it will soon slaughter the objects of her desire?

The eagle's identification of the geese with the suitors seems quite far-fetched, indeed. All that we know about the geese in the dream is that they are twenty, eat wheat, and are thoroughly domesticated. In contrast, the 106 suitors are thoroughly unruly carnivores. The beloved pet geese are much more likely to symbolize the happiness that Penelope finds in the home of her married life. As for the number twenty, its most powerful association in the *Odyssey* is first and foremost to the number of years that Odysseus has been gone, the years that the eagles of Atreus have snatched away. "In the twentieth year" is a frequent refrain. Thus, the waking anxiety that motivates the dream is Penelope's anxiety over having to give up her beloved home of twenty years. By leaving her house and her present marriage, Penelope abandons the last hope of reunion with Odysseus. Moreover, in a single act, she would obliterate twenty years of hard-won *kleos*. It may be her duty to go away, but Penelope will depart with nothing that she loves.

The Cretan Interprets

Penelope now turns to the Cretan for an opinion. He answers:

> Lady, it is impossible to read this dream and avoid it
> by turning another way, since Odysseus himself has told you
> its meaning, how it will end. The suitors' doom is evident
> for one and all. Not one will avoid his death and destruction.
>
> (Od. 19.555–58)

In an uncharacteristic (and even comic) twist, the wily and compulsive bender of reality finds no urge to alter or embellish this dream. Voicing the probable sympathies of the epic's audience, the Cretan urges Penelope to relax and wait, to be a little less *apistos*.

Penelope's dream should remind the reader of the bird omen in book 15, since it is similar in structure and interpretation. Just as Telemachos was about to leave Sparta, "a bird flew by on the right, an eagle, carrying in his talons a great white goose he had caught tame from the yard" (15.160–62). The eagle's flight is taken as an omen, and Menelaos is called on to explain it. Menalaos, however, is too slow to respond. Helen, ever ready to accommodate, interprets instead.

> [S]o Odysseus, after wandering long and suffering
> much, will come home and take revenge; or he is already
> home, and making a plan of evil for all of the suitors.
>
> (15.176–78)

At first blush, the parallel seems to hint almost at a standard code of interpretation, aimed at insuring that we can embrace the Cretan's endorsement of the dream's self-interpretation. Nevertheless, once we take into account who interprets the omen at Sparta, we are forced to a very different conclusion. Helen proves unreliable in these matters. "Hear me!" she says, "I shall be your prophet, the way the immortals put it into my heart, and I think it will be accomplished" (15.172–73). What immortals could these be? Athene has just visited Telemachos to warn him and urge him on, yet she did not see fit to breathe a word about Odysseus. So there is no reason for her to have inspired the omen. What other god would have intervened at this point?

Because she knows how to beguile, Helen's intervention in anything is dangerous. For instance, in Troy's last hours, she nearly
wrecked the scheme of the wooden horse by counterfeiting the voices
of the wives of all the various men who were hidden in it; if it had not
been for Odysseus's discipline and strong hands (as Menelaos reveals in
book 4 of the *Odyssey*), the Greeks would have been discovered and
slaughtered. How did Helen manage to delude every man but Odysseus? More to the point, how could these hardened warriors—sepa-
rated from their families by a wide sea and from death by a few thin
boards—have deluded themselves into believing that their wives were
within easy reach, except through a deep wish to believe and Helen's
extraordinary talent for accommodating and exploiting wishes? Helen
is the master broker of escapism—of the pleasant, the unreal, the
merely wishful. She administers the dreamy drug.[11]

> Into the wine of which they were drinking she cast a medicine
> of heartease, free of gall, to make one forget all sorrows,
> and whoever had drunk it down once it had been mixed in the
>   wine bowl,
> for the day that he drank it would have no tear roll down his
>   face,
> not if his mother died and his father died, not if men
> murdered a brother or a beloved son in his presence
> with the bronze, and he his own eyes saw it.
>
> (4.220–26)

Helen's drug could make even the daughter of Pandareos cheerful.
Penelope knows from Eumaios that the vagabond trucks in deceit, and
she has more or less promised him that she will not believe a word.
Even so, she oddly tells Eumaios that she will reward the vagabond
with beautiful clothing, "if I learn that everything he says is truthfully
spoken" (17.549). More oddly yet, after she gives him her test, Penelope decides to disclose her deepest secrets to the Cretan, and one cannot shake the feeling that she does so because she comes to trust the
man to speak truthfully.

The word that Lattimore translates as "truthfully" is *nēmertea*.
What sort of truth does this word imply? Five of the twenty-seven
times it is used in the *Odyssey*, it is the epithet of Proteus, the Old Man
of the Sea. The episode with Proteus, which involves the problem of

how to wrestle and pin down the ever-changing form in order to question it, is emblematic of the *Odyssey* itself.[12] Eidothea, Proteus's daughter, gives Menelaos instructions on how to handle her father. Changing from shape to slippery shape, the old man will make capture difficult, but once pinned down, he will remain docile and will offer his knowledge, presumably in goodwill. His knowledge, though, is not prophetic.[13] It is knowledge of the past (4.495–537), the present happening in other places (4.555–60), the possible (4.547), or the conditional (4.475–80). His only prediction of the future is the highly problematic one that Menelaos will never die but will live a blissful eternal life romping through the Elysian fields.[14]

Penelope decides to solicit the Cretan's advice precisely because he proves his goodwill and demonstrates his intention to place her interests above his. One of the ways he does this is to refuse the gifts that she offers. He seems to tell his story without ulterior motives, for Penelope's pleasure alone. He is not in it for the money.

> O respected wife of Odysseus, son of Laertes,
> coverlets and shining rugs have been hateful to me
> ever since that time when I left the snowy mountains
> of Crete behind me, and went away on my long-oared vessel.
> I will lie now as I have lain before through the sleepless
> nights; for many have been the nights when on an unpleasant
> couch I lay and awaited the throned Dawn in her splendor.
> Nor is there any desire in my heart for foot basins. . . .
>
> (19.336–43)

Penelope makes her evaluation of the Cretan at the end of their first fireside conversation.

> Dear friend, never before has there been any man so artless
>   [*pepnumenos*],
> among those friends from far places who have come to my
>   palace
> as guests, so artless [*pepnumena*] and so well-considered[15] is
>   everything you say.
>
> (19.350–52)

Especially interesting about this passage is the use of *pepnumenos* (and *pepnumena*—the plural neuter noun having, in effect, the same force as the adjective). The real Odysseus is distinctly not *pepnumenos*, that is, not artless. Perhaps, only the truly artful can feign artlessness.

The only other character to refer to Odysseus as artless is Alkinoös, the king of Phaiakia, and, like Penelope, he does so before he knows who he is talking to. Alkinoös uses the word (*pepnumenos* at 8.388, *pepnumena* at 8.586) as an explanation of why friendly—even brotherly—trust ought to be extended toward the stranger. His trust of the stranger who has mysteriously appeared at his court comes when he witnesses the stranger's ability to feel deeply for others. The story that the Phaiakian bard tells is of the destruction of Troy, and the stranger is overcome with emotion.

> So the famous singer sang his tale, but Odysseus
> melted, and from under his eyes the tears ran down, drenching
>   his cheeks.
> As a woman weeps, lying over the body
> of her dear husband. . .
>
> (8.521–24)

The message is that Odysseus is weeping not for himself but for the lost ones of both sides. Finding that the stranger's feelings are generous, Alkinoös becomes confident that he will react toward the Phaiakians as a sympathetic friend. Then, in the last words of book 8, which are the last words before Odysseus reveals his identity, Alkinoös defines friendship.

> Or could it then have been some companion, a brave man
>   knowing
> thoughts gracious toward you, since one who is your
>   companion, and has
> artless[16] thoughts toward you, is of no less degree than a
>   brother?
>
> (8.584–86)

Penelope turns to the Cretan, then, not for his knowledge but for his empathy and goodwill. Once she has pinned him down, she can trust him to tell her nothing but pleasing things that he believes will be of help. One might say that she trusts the artlessness of his art.

The Cretan's interpretation of the dream is indeed very accommodating, and Penelope would welcome it, if she could. Rejecting it will only invite great pain for her now and for a long time to come: ". . . forsaking this house where I was a bride, a lovely place and full of good living. I think that even in my dreams I shall never forget it" (19.579–81).

Why, then, does Penelope categorically reject the Cretan's advice, advice that she solicited and genuinely welcomes and that is seemingly artless, accommodating, and pleasant? Can there be any valid grounds for her decision?

Penelope Interprets

Penelope's own interpretation of the dream of the geese begins at *Odyssey* 19.560. She notes, "dreams are things hard to interpret, hopeless to puzzle out, and people find that not all of them end in anything" (19.560–61). In other words, some dreams are false or deceptive, promising things that will never come true, while other dreams are true. Penelope explains this in her famous and original theory of the origin of dreams.

> There are two gates through which the insubstantial dreams
>   issue.
> One pair of gates is made of horn, and one of ivory.
> Those of the dreams which issue through the gate of sawn
>   ivory,
> these are deceptive dreams, their message is never
>   accomplished.
> But those that come into the open through the gates of the
>   polished
> horn accomplish the truth for any mortal who see them.
>   (19.562–67)

This altogether reasonable theory runs immediately into an epistemological wall. No dreamer knows through which gate any dream comes unless the dream makes it known. At the same time, no dream can communicate reliable information about what gate it has come through unless the dreamer knows from an independent source the gate through which the dream has emerged.[17] Treated as a purely linguistic structure, the dream is ultimately inscrutable.

One way for the dream to be unreliable is for it to be sent by a lying god. Another way is for the dream to have no divine origin at all. Despite Freud's insistence to the contrary, ancient Greeks could differentiate dreams on the basis of whether their origin was outside or inside the mind.[18] As Dodds points out (1951, 107), we know that Herophilus distinguished between god-sent and wish-fulfillment dreams in the third century BCE. It may be, then, that Penelope's dream is the expression of an acute, intolerable anxiety and that the motive for the eagle's return and interpretation of the dream is to relieve that very anxiety.[19] There is critical support for this view. Dodds writes: "Again, in Penelope's dream of the eagle and the geese in *Odyssey* 19 we have a simple wish-fulfilment dream with symbolism and what Freud calls 'condensation' and 'displacement'" (106). C. Emlyn-Jones argues that the entire dream is driven by a wish to be taken care of, to be rid of responsibility.

> On a psychological level, it is surely more plausible to see Penelope's dream, as related at 19.535–53, as pure wish-fulfillment; her dream and her account of it is an expression, *not* of her belief or suspicion about the identity of the beggar but of her intense desire that Odysseus should come and extricate her from a terrible situation. (1984, 4)

Both Dodds and Emlyn-Jones are correct as far as their evaluations go. Where they fall short is in assuming that their interpretations would be news to Penelope.

Penelope seems to understand that the second part of her dream might well be a desperate attempt to lull her own self into believing that the core dream is not an unpleasant one; that, rather, it is as beautiful as carved ivory; and that through it all, her problems will miraculously evaporate without the slightest pain or effort. Such a dream would be welcome if it were not a self-deception. Still, Penelope has no conclusive evidence that her dream is not what it claims to be. Successful interpretation requires the kind of careful self-scrutiny of slippery motives that is all but logically impossible. Penelope does her best by turning to the Cretan, not as a soothsayer or oneiromancer, but as a storyteller, a kind of benevolent confidence man, professionally adept at discerning and exploiting a latent desire. She uses him as a touchstone of her wishes—not so she may follow them, but so she may resist them.

PENELOPE'S LAST DREAM

We can apply what we have so far learned to Penelope's last dream, a dream that has otherwise baffled analysis. The night after Penelope reports the dream of the twenty geese to Odysseus, her nightmares become so much worse that she prays to Artemis for release from them, even if it must be in death:[20] "But now the god has sent the evil dreams thronging upon me" (*Od.* 20.87). Paradoxically, the horrible nightmare she cites is a vivid dream of unmitigated joy.

> For on this very night there was one who lay by me, like him
> as he was when he went with the army, so that my own heart
> was happy. I thought it was no dream, but a waking vision.
> (20.88–90)

Penelope would indeed be happy to lie beside Odysseus, even, as she says, among the shades: "Artemis strike me, so that I could meet the Odysseus I long for, even under the hateful earth, and not have to please the mind of an inferior husband" (20.80–82).

Now that the sweet wish has taken over her sleep and even managed to shed its dreaminess and present itself as reality, as a waking vision, why should Penelope be distressed? What is so evil about a pleasant dream?[21] Pleasant daydreams were enough for Telemachos in book 1. The answer, I think, is that the evil lies not with the pleasure or with the wish for the pleasure but with the consequence of being beguiled by it. At *Odyssey* 20.88, the verb for "lay beside" is *paredrathen*. Homer employs it just one other time, at *Iliad* 14.163, when Hera connives to beguile Zeus and thwart his will by lying with him, satisfying him, and lulling him to sleep. The nightmare is Penelope's glimpse of the power of illusion and self-delusion, the seduction into the wished-for reality, the forgetting of the pain that is real life. She fears that her own mind is slipping her drams of Helen's drug.

Her crying leads us, so to speak, right to Odysseus, who overhears it in his sleep and integrates it into his own anxieties and second thoughts. He envisions his wife standing beside him and recognizing him. The fight is already over. This is what Odysseus wishes for. Once awake, he begs Zeus for an auspicious sign. Zeus sends two. What would have happened if the signs were not forthcoming? Penelope gets none. She is left quite alone.

PENELOPE'S HEROISM

It is important to be clear about exactly what Penelope has accomplished. She has been powerfully tempted by her own wishful thinking, but she has managed to discern the wish and resist the temptation. She flatly refuses to be deceived by her own desires, no matter how strong they are or how plausible the excuses they generate may be made to seem. It would be lovely for Penelope if, on the strength of the recent predictions by the sympathetic beggar and by Theoklymenos, she could excuse herself for a while from the painful necessity of remarriage. But that would be irresponsible. It is to Penelope's great credit that she faces her responsibility squarely. She will not be conned. In the end, whether or not her dream has come through the gate of horn or through the gate of ivory, Penelope knows that she cannot take the chance. The stakes are too high.

The dramatic irony that Homer employs so skillfully throughout the *Odyssey* to engage and challenge the reader is here especially intense. We know that reality is about to take a sudden turn in Penelope's favor. But this hardly means that she is making a mistake. We, the audience, who know more, are placed in a relationship with Penelope that is characteristic of tragedy. We long to cry out to her: "Please Penelope, believe the beggar! Believe the dream! Delay a few more days, at least."

At the very moment, then, that Penelope rises to her greatest stature by stubbornly doing the right thing, she induces bitter criticisms of infidelity, irrationality, passivity, confusion, lack of integrity, foolishness, deception, and self-delusion. Nevertheless, this is exactly the moment that she proves herself above every one of these charges. If, in the process, she leaves the audience morally gaping, so much more wonderful is the dramatic moment. Instead of competing with Odysseus for the crown of deception, Penelope should get laurels for being the most resistant to being deceived.

PENELOPE'S TRAGEDY

I have purposely delayed discussing one of the most powerful pressures on Penelope. In book 19, after Penelope has heard the Cretan's skillful account of himself and Odysseus, Penelope arranges a few comforts for her affable guest. As she orders a bed to be made and a footbath to be drawn, she emphasizes that she does all these things out of concern for her own *kleos* (fame, reputation, glory): "For how, my friend, will you learn if I in any way surpass the rest of women, in mind and thoughtful good sense" (*Od.* 19.325–26).

Like any Homeric character, she is—and should be—concerned with her *kleos*. Unlike other Homeric characters, she is extremely articulate about exactly what *kleos* is. Her last words before sending Odysseus to Eurykleia to get his feet scrubbed eloquently expose the Homeric philosophy of *kleos* and its overwhelming importance to the individual.

> Human beings live for only a short time,
> and when a person is harsh herself, and her mind knows harsh
>   thoughts,
> all mortals pray that sufferings will befall her hereafter
> while she lives; and when she is dead all make fun of her.
> But when a person is blameless herself, and her thoughts are
>   blameless,
> the friends she has entertained carry her fame widely
> to all humanity, and many are they who call her excellent.[22]
>   (19.328–34)

As a mere expansion on Penelope's desire for her guest to be comfortable in the house, this philosophical meditation is a bit much; as a sign, however, that she is acutely aware of the importance of *kleos* and has begun to concentrate on the tragedy of her situation, it is not. The double use of *apēnēs* (harsh)[23] at *Odyssey* 19.329 helps to focus the meditation on Penelope herself. Though the only previous use of the word occurs when the Cretan beggar rebukes Eurymachos, who then tosses a stool at the poor man (18.381), the only instances of the word after book 19 apply exclusively to Penelope. If it is not going too far to discern the phonological root of her own name in the word, we might see how Penelope further focuses the discussion of *kleos* on herself, insisting that the person who does not merit *kleos*—who is *a-pēnes*—is not her.

Penelope is left at the fireside pondering her *kleos* as Eurykleia bathes Odysseus's feet and suddenly recognizes the scar. *Kleos* is the underlying theme of the famous digression that follows. The account of the boar hunt and Odysseus's wound is too well known to need retelling here. It is the longest account of an event told directly by the narrator. We ought to take it as something like the unadulterated story, tradition within tradition, exemplifying the sort of eternal fame that Penelope has just been talking about. The indelible scar demonstrates the sheer power of *kleos*. Upon getting a glimpse of it, Eurykleia wells over with admiration and love. Odysseus's reputation is one that can hardly be contained, even when he wants it to be.

By definition, Penelope's *kleos* depends on what the people say about her and what they hold to be virtuous action. She tells us that her *kleos* would get its biggest boost if Odysseus were to vindicate her long wait by a triumphant return home. Barring that, what *kleos* she enjoys flows from her obstinate refusal of other men. The worst thing that Penelope could do for her *kleos* is just what she is called on to do. We get a glimpse of the probable Ithacan reaction to what she plans to do—when they think that she has already done it. They call her *schetliē*, wicked, cruel woman (23.150). There is great irony hidden in this word. Here, it is pejorative, but the ameliorative sense is "tenacious, tough, stubborn." According to Chantraine, the original sense is from the verb *echō* and means "holding out to the very end."[24] The Ithacan accusation, however, is that Penelope is not holding out as she should: "She had no patience to keep the great house for her own wedded lord to the end, till he came back to her" (23.150–51). The Ithacans have gotten the virtue right but not its manifestation. The noble and courageous choice will win Penelope disdain or, worse, oblivion.

Heroes are heroes because they make the hard choice that no one else can. In return for their heroism, they win *kleos*. But Penelope will not. For her, heroism demands the courage to go unrecognized as a hero. I call this tragic. No one else in the Homeric epics is called on to make such a great sacrifice.

CHAPTER FIVE

The Limits of Deception

"Wake, Penelope, dear child"—these are the first words from the elderly Eurykleia when she comes up to Penelope's room laughing—practically dancing—with the news that Odysseus has returned and slaughtered every last one of the suitors. This is news that, according to Eurykleia, Penelope has longed for so long. But Penelope resents being disturbed from the sweetest sleep she has had in twenty years.

We can see why Penelope might want another hour in bed, now that she has made her decision and should be free from guilty or tempting nightmares. At the same time, this may be the last night she spends in her own bed. In any case, she certainly has no compelling reason to rush into a day that will only reveal to her a new, inevitably loathsome husband. Penelope also wonders whether the gods have scrambled Eurykleia's normally level head. The gods, Penelope insists, can do it to anyone, if they choose.

> They are both able
> to change a very sensible person into a senseless
> one, and to set the light-wit on the way of discretion.
> They have set you awry; before now your thoughts were
> orderly.[1]
>
> (*Od.* 23.11–14)

Eurykleia insists that her report is the simple truth and that Telemachos can confirm it. Suddenly—as if she were only just now fully awake—Penelope springs up in joy at the possibility. Encouraged, Eurykleia expands on what she heard and saw. She exhorts Penelope to go downstairs to her long-suffering, but triumphant, husband and accept the happiness that she can now enjoy with him. Again she reminds Penelope that this has always been her wish ("Now at last what long you prayed for has been accomplished," 23.54), and Penelope confirms her longing in words very similar to those she has used so often before to answer prophecies of Odysseus's return: "You know how welcome he would be if he appeared in the palace: to all, but above all to me and the son we gave birth to" (23.60–61).

Nevertheless, contrary to Eurykleia's expectations, Penelope concludes, "No, but this story is not true as you tell it" (23.62). Penelope doesn't doubt the fact of a slaughter, merely who is responsible. Eurykleia is too trustworthy to intentionally misrepresent such a gross fact, and Penelope is too practical to deny it. In Penelope's mind, though, it is unlikely that Odysseus is responsible. It is more likely, from her point of view, that the gods themselves have extracted justice on their own account for the "wicked deeds [kaka erga] and heart-hurting violence [hubrin thumalgea]" of the suitors. So, Penelope holds firm to the kind of skeptical reasoning that she so forcefully and commendably applied in book 19. To her, Eurykleia's report is like a dream that has slipped through the gate of ivory: it would be sweet if it were true, but wishing does not make it so. Penelope is determined not to be seduced out of the one thing that she considers most likely to be true: "But Odysseus has lost his homecoming and lost his life, far from Achaia" (23.68–69). Has Penelope's resistance gone too far?

Eurykleia is exasperated, and so, I think, is the epic audience. There is no question for the audience that Odysseus is home and has slaughtered the suitors. Book 22 is no dream for us. What earlier appeared to be a virtue in Penelope now seems to border on perversion. Has she gone mad? Did we give her too much credit for good motivations? Did we wrongly applaud what seemed like intelligent resistance but was in fact only constitutional obstinacy? Is she now really deceiving herself? At the very least, is Penelope carrying her mistrust too far? Homer has engineered the scene so that these worries come spontaneously. He further promotes our disappointment with Penelope through Eurykleia's next scolding words, through Penelope's attitude toward the scar, and through Telemachos's indignant speech to his mother.

Though Penelope has previously discounted all reports of Odysseus's return, apparently with Eurykleia's approval, the old nurse now argues that it is no longer wise to be so *apistos* as to insist that Odysseus will never return—since he already has: "But you were always unbelieving, and have made up your mind that your husband is never coming, although he is in this house" (23.71–72; trans. Butler).

As I pointed out earlier, in chapter 4, *apistos* shifts its meaning from the *Iliad* to the *Odyssey*. But here, the Iliadic connotation shades its use. Penelope's all but rabid skepticism makes her "not to be trusted," even "faithless." E. V. Rieu's 1945 translation hints at this: "Here is your husband at his own fireside, and you declare he never will get home. What little faith you always had!" Could it be that in the final analysis, Penelope is not to be trusted to face reality, to accept what she has so longed for, or to continue her loyalty to her husband? Is she breaking faith, acting irrationally? Could she even be preparing some deception of her own? The *Iliad*'s vice, which became a virtue in the *Odyssey*, is now, because of excess, threatening to revert.

More disturbing yet may be Penelope's rejection of the scar as proof of Odysseus's identity. Three loyal people have accepted the scar as incontrovertible evidence, and Homer has established its reality in one of the most famous digressions in all literature. In book 23, Eurykleia, swearing to Penelope that she has recognized the scar, offers an oath on her very life as guarantee (23.78–79). Penelope's own words seem to betray her when she lightly rejects the oath,[2] saying merely, "Dear nurse, it would be hard for you to baffle[3] the purposes of the everlasting gods, although you are very clever" (23.81–82).

Penelope consents to descend to the great hall to view the triumphant stranger and the slaughter that he has achieved. When her eyes fall on him, she is nonplussed, dumbstruck (*aneō* [23.93]). Telemachos, taking his mother's silence as a sign of mulishness, launches into a bitter diatribe against her, beginning, "My mother, my harsh mother with the hard heart inside you . . ." (23.97). These are bitter words of denunciation. The word translated by Lattimore as "my harsh mother" is the ugly and impious *dusmēter*. Not only does this word not appear anywhere else in Homer; it finds virtually no other occasion for employment in extant Greek literature.[4] Liddell and Scott translate this half line: "My mother, yet no mother . . ."

In the second half of the line Telemachos accuses his mother of having a hard heart inside of her. The word that Lattimore translates with "hard" is *apēnea*, the word that Penelope used in book 19 in her speech on *kleos* and which I discussed briefly in my last chapter. It is again tempting to hear a punning reference to Penelope's own name so that the thrust of this line might be expanded into something like: "Mother, you are out of your mind and no longer recognizable to me as my mother or no doubt to yourself as who you ought to be." Just like Eurykleia, Telemachos finds no excuse in Penelope's reticence. He, too, is exasperated and blurts out:

> Why do you withdraw so from my father, and do not
> sit beside him and ask him questions and find out about him?
> No other woman, with spirit as stubborn as yours, would keep
>   back
> as you are doing from her husband who, after much suffering,
> came at last in the twentieth year back to his own country.
> But always you have a heart that is harder than stone within you.
>
> (23.98–103)

For his part, Odysseus initially remains cool. Smiling the Homeric smile of superiority at his son's excess, Odysseus calmly assures Telemachos that he knows his own wife. The problem, he says, is no more than a matter of what he is wearing: "but now that I am dirty and wear foul clothing upon me, she dislikes me for that, and says I am not her husband" (23.115–16). So, Odysseus goes off to be bathed, oiled, and spruced by Eurykleia and then glorified by Athene. He is confident that this will do the trick.

> [A]nd over his head Athene suffused great beauty, to make
>   him
> taller to behold and thicker, and on his head she arranged
> the curling locks that hung down like hyacinthine petals.
> ·
> Then, looking like an immortal, he strode forth from the bath.
>
> (23.156–63)

But, returning to his wife, Odysseus quickly discovers the inadequacy of his condescending assessment of her. Penelope is not fooled by his fresh look. This is too much for the man of many wiles. Suddenly losing his composure, he is reduced to repeating the very same reproach that he had chuckled at when his son leveled it sixty-eight lines earlier.

No other woman, with spirit as stubborn as yours, would keep
    back
as you are doing from her husband who, after much suffering,
came at last in the twentieth year back to his own country.

(23.168–70)

Paradoxically, Penelope's reaction—or lack of it—is the very reason that some critics reject the scene as a post-Homeric interpolation.
Heubeck argues, "This [scene] is obviously in contrast to the normal
development of this form of typical scene; in such circumstances it is
usual to mention the effect of the transformation of appearance on the
other person . . . and then for the other party to make some comment
on the change" (Russo 1992, 329). It is true that the two other occasions on which Athene radically transforms Odysseus's appearance
elicit strong responses. In book 6, Nausicaa says: "A while ago he
seemed an unpromising man to me. Now he even resembles one of the
gods, who hold high heaven" (6.242–43). In book 16, Telemachos reacts with fear as well as admiration:

Suddenly you have changed, my friend, from what you were
    formerly;
your skin is no longer as it was, you have other clothing.
Surely you are one of the gods who hold the high heaven.
Be gracious, then: so we shall give you favored offerings
and golden gifts that have been well wrought. Only be
    merciful.

(16.181–85)

Clearly, as Heubeck points out, the pattern is for such changes to make
a strong impression on those who witness the results. But the consequence of any pattern is a heightened awareness of its absence. In
Penelope's case and in general, the epic formula possesses a sort of potential energy that the poet can exploit.[5] Such potential may even be
one of the principal reasons that the formula is employed in the first
place. What better way is there to emphasize that Penelope is not awed
by appearance or cowed by fear, even fear of the gods?

The transformation scene is rejected by some as un-Homeric because it disappoints the expectations of the epic audience; others reject
it as a sheer waste of the audience's time. Dawe, who prints it in smaller

type to show that he thinks it spurious, comments: "[Odysseus] now returns from the bath resplendent in beauty but the change is quite un-
noticed . . . . We do not need this transformation" (1993, 816). True,
we do not need Odysseus's transformation in order to sway Penelope's
opinion. We do need it, however, to discover what Penelope is about.

In book 23, Homer engineers one of his most impressive narrative
effects. Even though, until this moment, Penelope was called on to act
heroically without the compensatory prospect of personal recognition
for it from the people in her world, at least Homer allowed her to enjoy
sympathy and affirmation from those outside—that is, from the epic
audience. At the beginning of book 23, however, the poet affords this
audience the bittersweet experience of being lured into abandoning
her. Eventually, when that same audience discovers that its reasons for
doubting Penelope—which looked so valid through the eyes of Eurykleia, Telemachos, and Odysseus—are unfounded, Penelope reclaims its
humblest respect.

PENELOPE RECONSIDERED

The first poetic hints of the countercurrent that gradually guides the
attentive audience to renewed respect for Penelope's position come at
least as early as Telemachos's diatribe against his *dusmēter*. In it, for instance, Telemachos's complaint that his mother has a heart harder
than stone (*kpadiē stereōterē lithoio*) is actually a transformed compliment. Remember that when Eurykleia assures Odysseus that she will
keep his secret, she says, "You know what strength is steady in me, and
it will not give way at all, but I shall hold as stubborn as stone or iron"
(*Od.* 19.493–94). More striking yet is the use of the phrase: "with spirit
as stubborn as yours" (*tetlēoti thumōi*). Though this phrase is meant to
serve as a stern rebuke of Penelope when used of her by Telemachos
(23.100) and Odysseus (23.168), every other use in the *Odyssey* is intended as high praise. Thus, Lattimore rightly translates the two uses
in book 23 as "with a stubborn spirit," while rendering all the other
seven occurrences in the poem with some variation of "with an enduring spirit." Outside of book 23, *tetlēoti thumōi* is clearly connected to
endurance and heroic determination. Menelaos uses the phrase twice
in the story of how he and his men subdued Proteus, their only hope
for returning home. The entire morning, Menelaos explains, hidden
under seal skins that stank terribly until the goddess sweetened them

with ambrosia, he and his men waited "with enduring spirit (4.447)" to ambush the god. When Proteus appears, they grab him and wrestle him as he transforms himself successively from a serpent, to a leopard, to a great boar, to moving water, to a mighty tree. Still, Menelaos and his men cling to the wild old man tenaciously, "with enduring spirit" (4.459). With equal tenacity—described by the same phrase—Odysseus clings to the ram's fleece to escape the Cyclops.

> I clasped [the ram] around the back, snuggled under the wool
>   of the belly,
> and stayed there still, and with a firm twist of the hands and
>   enduring
> spirit clung fast to the glory of this fleece, unrelenting.
>   (9.433–35)

Both Antikleia and Eumaios apply the phrase *tetlēoti thumōi* to Penelope with admiration (11.181, 16.37). Finally, Odysseus, in his great assessment of the human condition, uses it to pinpoint humankind's redeeming virtue.

> Of all creatures that breathe and walk on the earth there is
>   nothing
> more helpless than a man is, of all that the earth fosters;
> for he thinks that he will never suffer misfortune in future
> days, while the gods grant him courage, and his knees have
>   spring
> in them. But when the blessed gods bring sad days upon him,
> against his will he must suffer it with enduring spirit.
>   (18.130–35)

When Penelope does not react as expected to the extreme makeover that Athene has given Odysseus, he cries out to his wife in exasperation, "*Daimoniē!*" (strange woman! 23.166). If Odysseus means to accuse his wife of acting under some divine influence, Penelope is quite correct to reverse the charge a few lines later by saying, "*Daimoniē,*" to him (23.174). After all, Athene is behind him, not behind Penelope. Even if Odysseus means simply to say that Penelope is acting—as we would say—irrationally, the charge is still more applicable to him than to her. This Cretan irrationally expects Penelope to accept as proof of his true identity a miraculous transformation wrought by one of the gods, none of whom (she could assure us) scruple to deceive a human mind.

To hear Penelope tell it, she is being completely reasonable: "I am not being proud, nor indifferent, nor puzzled beyond need" (23.174–75). There are good reasons to believe these three claims. That Penelope is initially dumbstruck (*aneō*) shows that she is far from indifferent (*out' atherizō*) about the outcome of these events. Her equanimity in the face of Odysseus's splendorous transformation shows that she was not merely being haughty (*out' ar ti megalizomai*). Her third claim (*oute liēn agamai*) is probably a more sweeping disclaimer meant to deny any admixture of awe, fear, or anger in her motives. (All of these charges have been made against Penelope through the ages.)[6] What, then, is Penelope's motivation, if it is not any of these? How can she justify her hesitation as a rational act?

After the recognition is successful, Penelope tells us exactly what was guiding her actions, and her statement is consistent with what we have seen of her all along. She was protecting the House of Odysseus by staying on the alert against impostors.

> Then do not now be angry with me nor blame me, because
> I did not greet you, as I do now, at first when I saw you.
> For always the spirit deep in my very heart was fearful
> that some one of mortal men would come my way and deceive
>   me
> with words. For there are many who scheme for wicked
>   advantage.
>
> (23.213–17)

I take these words seriously not only as a sincere explanation of Penelope's motivations but as an accurate assessment of the danger to her family. A successful usurper would surely spell the end of the House of Odysseus. However avid Telemachos might be in his belief that the man who has just slaughtered his enemies is his father, that man is unlikely to privilege him as his son if he is not.

RECOGNITION AND ITS PROBLEMS

Every recognition scene involves a test, and every test implies some evidentiary standard. The standard will vary from genre to genre, from work to work, and even between two scenes of a single work. Among other things, the standard will depend on what is at risk to the characters and on the thematic goal of the author. Sometimes the standard is quite high, as in the *Oedipus Tyrannus*; at other times, it is quite low, illogical, or merely symbolic. A strand of hair or even a footprint that is unrealistically supposed to be commensurate between a brother and a sister might do.

In a fairy tale, a glass slipper will fit no other than the one special foot. Likewise, recognitions in the Homeric poems are generally as intellectually unproblematic as they are emotionally profound. A fine example is the iconic mutual recognition of master and dog. Argos, the loyal and once fine hound, now lying near death on a dung pile, recognizes his master and makes a final, feeble gesture of contentment.

> [H]e wagged his tail, and laid both his ears back; only
> he now no longer had the strength to move any closer
> to his master, who, watching him from a distance, without
>   Eumaios
> noticing, secretly wiped a tear away.
>
> (17.302–5)

The recognition between father and son in the previous book was more emotional yet.

> So he spoke, and sat down again, but now Telemachos
> folded his great father in his arms and lamented,
> shedding tears, and desire for mourning rose in both of them;
> and they cried shrill in pulsing voice, even more than the
>   outcry
> of birds, ospreys or vultures with hooked claws, whose children
> were stolen away by the men of the fields, before their wings
>   grew
> strong; such was their pitiful cry and the tears their eyes wept.
>
> (16.213–19)

The evidentiary standard that Telemachos employs to test whether the stranger standing before him is really the long-lost father that he has never seen could hardly be more lax. Naturally, Telemachos's first thought is that this Cretan beggar who has just been utterly transfigured on the spot must surely be a god. The Cretan replies: "No, I am not a god. Why liken me to the immortals? But I am your father" (16.187–88). Telemachos holds back long enough to show that he knows the risks involved: "No, you are not Odysseus my father, but some divinity beguiles me, so that I must grieve the more, and be sorry" (16.194–95). To that objection, the Cretan offers a simple and winning response:

> Telemachos, it does not become you to wonder too much
> at your own father when he is here, nor doubt him. No other
> Odysseus than I will ever come back to you. But here I am. . . .
>
> (16.202–4)

"No other Odysseus than I will ever come back to you"—this is proof enough for Telemachos, who falls into his father's arms, weeps, and believes.

This scene recalls the meeting of Nausicaa and Odysseus in book 6 on the Scherian beach, which has the structure of a recognition scene: Nausicaa recognizes Odysseus as her future husband. Athene transforms Odysseus and Nausicaa is mightily impressed. Nausicaa, of course, is mistaken; this is not her future husband standing before her. The mistake is made plausible not least by Athene's involvement. She has deceived Nausicaa, or rather, abetted Nausicaa's own vulnerability to self-deception in order to make it easier for her favorite hero to succeed. Both Nausicaa and Telemachos show themselves to be rather callow (*nēpios*). They accept as true what they wish were.

There are two further recognition scenes prior to that between husband and wife, and both rest on the tangible evidence of the scar on Odysseus's thigh. Eurykleia recognizes her former master by this scar. So do Eumaios and Philotios. When Odysseus shows the scar to them, they are unreservedly ready to obey. In book 23, Eurykleia again treats the scar as absolute proof of Odysseus's identity. As I have argued earlier, Homer has established the scar as such solid evidence of Odysseus's identity that it is shocking to see Penelope ignore it. Nevertheless, she does, and this forces further reflection on its probative value.

How identifiable is any scar, really? Would the application of a scar be too much for a goddess who has affected the numerous and profound changes of Odysseus that we have already seen? Would a wound in the thigh be uncommon for hunters of animals with horns or tusks? Modern bullfighters, for example, are gored most often in just that place. And I suppose that one cannot easily distinguish a hunting wound from a war wound, or remember very accurately the precise character of any scar after twenty years. Scars do fade over time. Furthermore, this scar might conceivably have been self-inflicted for the very purpose of deception. Think of the account in Herodotus of Zopyrus, who "cut off his nose and ears and shaved his hair to disfigure himself, and laid lashes on himself,"[7] all so that he could deceive the Babylonians into believing that he was a traitor to Darius, his king. The imposture worked for Zopyrus, and he won himself the rule of Babylon, tax-free, for the rest of his life. Odysseus, Helen tells us, "flagellated himself with degrading strokes" in order to slip into Troy on reconnaissance (*Od.* 4.244).

While Penelope can expect little sympathy for her strict standard of proof from other members of the household who have accepted a less rigorous one, the epic audience is forced to admit that Penelope has a good point. We can hardly encourage Penelope to endorse the stranger simply because no other Odysseus is likely to come back to her or because the man physically resembles the one who went away to Troy. By raising the possibility of a higher standard of proof, the poet focuses attention on the idea of recognition itself and links it to the thematic concerns of the poem. How is it possible to keep from being deceived in a world where deception is a virtue and an art?

The pressures on Penelope are tremendous. She now believes that all the suitors have been miraculously killed by one man, possibly a total stranger, obviously with the endorsement—if not the direct intervention—of the gods. The stranger claims to be Odysseus, and no one but Penelope has any doubts about it. Her own son is ready to denounce her for any hesitation whatsoever. If, however, this stranger is not Odysseus—if he is an impostor—Telemachos is at great risk. In fact, Penelope's acceptance of an impostor could be far worse than her marriage to a suitor.

A Penelope concerned only with her own personal comfort and security, would understandably, and perhaps even wisely, embrace the victorious stranger without hesitation. On the one hand, this stranger enjoys de facto power in the house, and there is really little chance that Penelope's obstinacy could do more than keep him from sleeping with her, if it could do that. At the same time, the struggle for the future of the House of Odysseus is not over. The stranger is in great and imminent danger from forces outside the palace, forces that Penelope's

obstinacy would effectively aid. "For," as the stranger impresses upon
Telemachos,

> when one has killed only one man in a community,
> and then there are not many avengers to follow, even
> so, he flees into exile, leaving kinsmen and country.
> But we have killed what held the city together, the finest
>   young
> men in Ithaka. It is what I would have you consider.
>
> (23.118–22)

Because of the pressures on him, the stranger can hardly afford to indulge anyone who might compromise his success.

Even if he is in a hurry, Odysseus wants and needs Penelope to recognize him and accept him, in order to watch the *oikos*. ("You look after
my possessions which are in the palace" (23.355) and stonewall the
Ithacans while he and Telemachos are preparing for the next battle.

> Presently, when the sun rises, there will be a rumor
> about the men who courted you, whom I killed in our palace.
> Then go to the upper chamber with your attendant women,
> and sit still, looking at no one, and do not ask any questions.
>
> (23.362–65)

Penelope's criticism of the miraculous transformation in Odysseus
that Athene has affected lies in the difficult half line: *mala d'eu oid'hoios
eēstha* (Herodotus 3.154; trans Grene.)[8] Samuel Butler translated this
passage, "But I remember well what kind of man you were when . . .";
Bates, "Well I know what you were once when . . ."; Rouse, "but I know
what manner of man you were when . . ." Unlike the case when Penelope's words are taken to refer to the physical, we are now concerned
about personal characteristics that are not supposed to change. Penelope could be taken as meaning that she has a solid and reliable grasp
of the kind of man Odysseus was and cannot be fooled into a false
recognition and that the stranger has not yet proven himself to be that
man. For starters, she might be suspicious of any man who thought that
his wife could be bought by a show of power and fine dress. Is this the
same man who gave her his parting directive and expected her to guard

the home? Would the true Odysseus not be the sort of man who would expect her to demand a better reason to capitulate than he has yet given her?

This raises the fascinating (and unanswerable) question of what Penelope would do if she discovered that this man standing before her had nothing of the character or ideology that Odysseus had when he left for Troy, if he were no longer the just man who had once ruled with a fair and mild hand, if he were no longer the man to place his son and the sanctity of the *oikos* above other concerns. What if, for instance, she discovered that he, too, had a plot to eliminate Telemachos? How much and in what way must Odysseus be like the Odysseus of twenty years ago? Must Odysseus have preserved the core of his character and essential loyalties to be accepted as the same man that he was when he left for Troy?[9]

Even if we put aside such questions and assume that Odysseus need only identify himself as the same physical self that left twenty years ago, there is still a monumental problem. The simple, ineluctable truth is that Odysseus has become a man unable—on the strongest logical and rational grounds—to give credible assurances of his own identity. He is now in the position of a Cretan who says, "Believe me, all Cretans are liars," or, perhaps more to the point, "Believe me, I am not the Cretan that I said I was when I said that I was a Cretan." How does the lover of lies convince us that he is not now lying? As I sketched out in my introductory chapter, Homer binds Odysseus's identity tightly to *mētis*, even to a sort of super-*mētis* that warrants him—and him alone—the epithet *polumētis*. The link is especially explicit and self-conscious in book 9, in Polyphemus's cave, through the elaborate paronomastic interweaving of *outis* and *mētis*. In a sense, Odysseus may very well be, as Peradotto wrote, "never more himself, *autos*, than when he is *Outis*" (1990, 161). The times at which he comes as close to himself as he can manage on his own are when he is playing the trickster, when he is in disguise, or when he is employing his genius for *mētis* to get what he needs—when he is "No man" or a con man. It should not negate Peradotto's insight into book 9 and the theme of identity to point out that in book 23, Homer performs a sort of thematic peripeteia in which Odysseus's defining virtue becomes a confining vice, in which his very identity prevents him from having one. Odysseus's identity, which has been the cause of so many troubles for others, is now the cause of his own: Polyphemus was trapped by the *outis* that is *mētis*; Odysseus now traps himself in the *mētis* that leaves him *outis*.

Penelope must be especially aware of the problem. After all, she recognizes the Cretan as a master seducer who can play on the wishful hopes and desires of those he encounters, and in book 19, she trusts him to tell her exactly what he thinks that she wants to hear. His words are guaranteed to aim at beguiling (*thelgein*). At the beginning of the interlude, Homer brings the theme of deception back into sharp focus for the audience. When Odysseus suggests giving Penelope a little time to come to her senses, Telemachos consents out of respect for his father's reputation for *mētis*.

> You must look to this yourself, dear father; for they say
> you have the best mind among men for craft, and there is
> no other man among mortal men who can contend with you.
>
> (*Od.* 23.124–26)

Odysseus then turns his attention to the implementation of an elaborate deception designed to gain time for arming his allies and for his own escape to his country estate: he locks the doors and stages a mock wedding festival. Likewise, his plan to win Penelope over by changing his appearance was thoroughly based in the spirit of deception.

THE TEST

Odysseus therefore cannot establish his identity on his own. It is up to Penelope to find a way to it. She does so with her own sort of deception—a deception different from most others in the *Odyssey*, not least because she does not proceed by telling Odysseus what he would like to hear. Recent criticism has tended to credit Penelope in the recognition scene with tricking the trickster, deceiving the deceiver, beating Odysseus at his own game. Lattimore's explanatory heading for this page of his translation is, "She tricks him into betraying himself." Nevertheless, neither "trick" nor "betray" are the best words here. The central fact of this scene is that Odysseus wants to be recognized and accepted, and he has no reason to be fussy about the terms. He loses nothing by being made to reveal the secret of the bed. Penelope is not tricking the trickster so much as attempting, as it were, to redeem him—to save him from himself. Perhaps we might say that she is un-weaving the web that he has woven around himself. Penelope's task is no easy one, since, as we have seen, no material evidence, not even the scar, is conclusive, and no knowledge, not even a supposed secret, is inviolable. In truth, any test of which Odysseus is conscious would be compromised by that very fact. So, instead of questioning him further, Penelope pretends to back off, ceding to him every right but the right to sleep in her chamber.

> Come then, Eurykleia, and make up a firm bed for him
> outside the well-fashioned chamber: that very bed that he himself
> built. Put the firm bed here outside for him, and cover it
> over with fleeces and blankets, and with shining coverlets.
>
> (*Od.* 23.177–80)

Odysseus's passion immediately gets the best of him. Angrily he says: "What you have said, dear lady, has hurt my heart deeply" (23.183).

What exactly has hurt Odysseus's heart deeply? It is tempting to think he is wounded by hints of adultery. Beds are, after all, metonymically connected to the sexual act, as this one will be at the end of this book. Nevertheless, the connection of a movable bed with adultery does not hold up. Penelope would not move the bed out into the hall—or anywhere else for that matter—if she wanted to share it with another man. The need for privacy would demand that she prefer the one place where no one but herself and one trusty maid (Aktor's daughter) ever goes or is allowed to go. Furthermore, if Odysseus were reacting in anger to the threat of adultery, I think that the long (sixteen-line) speech that carefully and lovingly details the construction of the bed would be rather superfluous and silly, if not downright stupid.

In the end, Odysseus's rage does not really depend on whether or not he thinks that Penelope has moved the bed. It is enough that she should forget that it, unlike all other beds, was built to be immovable. He is fundamentally hurt that she should forget such an important secret, and she is relieved to see that he has not. No one but Odysseus would have taken so much care to build his bed so carefully and solidly, and no one but Odysseus would still be so emotionally tied to it as he shows himself to be. Therefore, Odysseus demonstrates that he continues to hold the values that he held when he made the bed to be the solid core of the *oikos*. I do not doubt that the bed is a symbol of marriage as well as a symbol of the stability of the *oikos*. After all is said and done, the marriage and the *oikos* are one. For Penelope, the marriage bond is a commitment to the House of Odysseus. What she has so stubbornly protected is her and Odysseus's heritage.

APOLOGY FOR HELEN

After Penelope establishes Odysseus's identity, she explains why she has been so careful and stubborn. Temptation is great, and knowledge is uncertain. Though all human beings might aim at doing what is good, their ability to succeed is naturally limited. Penelope cites Helen as a potent example.

> For neither would the daughter born to Zeus, Helen of Argos,
> have lain in love with an outlander from another country,
> if she had known that the warlike sons of the Achaians would
>   bring her
> home again to the beloved land of her fathers.
> It was a god who stirred her to do the shameful thing she
> did, and never before had she had in her heart this terrible
> wildness, out of which came suffering to us also.
>
> (*Od.* 23.218–24)

Since this speech is arguably the most limelit in the entire *Odyssey* (if for no other reason than its dramatic placement), it seems almost comical how many ancient and modern philologists reject these seven lines as spurious. Heubeck mentions Aristarchus, Kirchhoff, Wilamowitz-Moellendorff, Finsler, van Leeuwen, Schwartz, Schadewaldt, and von der Mühll (1992, 336–37). And these philologists do not reject the lines on firm textual grounds, but because they have not been able to fathom what purpose the lines have where they are placed. The sentiment has struck them as inapposite, illogical, or just plain nonsense. Here is a case in which Penelope's words are not discounted by the claim that she is lying; rather, they are discounted by the claim that she could never have said them.

Even many scholars who accept the speech as authentic have trouble with it. Roisman, in her 1987 article "Penelope's Indignation," attempts to salvage Penelope's apology for Helen by interpreting it as a subtle expression of Penelope's "hurt pride" and anger at Odysseus for being left out of the loop (68): "she greets her husband not with unalloyed delight, but rather with mixed feelings provoked by Odysseus's earlier treatment of her" (59). "The analogy she draws between her own experience and Helen's," Roisman goes on to argue, "which implies that there was no motive for her fidelity to Odysseus beyond her knowledge that he would someday come back and make her remarriage useless, is simply another cutting statement that expresses her anger" (68). I hope that I have dispelled any tendency to embrace this sort of argument, which inevitably reduces Penelope to a minor character with petty motives and little positive agency in the plot.

To my mind, with the apology for Helen, the poem attains a sublime height of grace and wisdom. The apology emphasizes not the power of the human seducers (Paris is not mentioned) but the weakness of the seduced—or, rather, the human propensity to self-deception. Penelope's analysis assumes the essentially Platonic point that no one who knows the truth does evil willingly, as well as the corollary to this point, namely, that the doer always believes the deed is for the best. Penelope's insight is that not even Helen, the most destructive of all women, intended to do evil. According to Penelope, Helen believed that she was making the right decision when she ran off with Paris and that all would work out well. The value of any decision, Penelope implies, depends on its consequences; but its consequences can never be known at the moment the decision is made. Helen would have had the strength to resist her act of wildness (*atē*) had she been able to foresee the future.

An incontrovertible fact of existence, though, is that no human can ever have certain knowledge of the future. From that fact flows all of life's permanent and ineluctable indeterminacy. In the face of the inescapable incompleteness of knowledge, it is the human tendency, for better or for worse, to fill in the gaps of knowledge with the imagination.

Except in the most steadfast of minds, the imagined outcome of any action is often the dupe of wishful thinking. In book 2 of the *Iliad*, Agamemnon, the supreme commander of the Greeks becomes as well a supreme symbol of one who is eager to fool himself. Zeus, who is himself vulnerable to seduction by Hera, successfully deceives him through a dream that can be compared to the one that Penelope refuses to believe. Zeus deliberately sends Agamemnon a lying dream that the epic audience knows is false and to which none of the other Greeks would have given the slightest credence had they dreamed it. The poet makes it clear that the leader of all the Achaians believes the dream to be true because he badly wishes it to be so. Would he have curbed himself, as Penelope says even Helen would, if he could have glimpsed the results?

Penelope has always been acutely aware of the risk of self-delusion and has always taken great pains—out of fear, she says—to resist it. For this reason, her vision is essentially tragic, though by no means sad or defeatist. She takes her responsibility seriously. Human action must be accomplished despite partial knowledge of exactly what is going on. This is the idea of the tragic that Helene Foley (1995) finds in both Aristotle and Penelope. It does not blame the gods for human suffering. In this, it invokes Zeus's lament in book 1 over the general stupidity of people who blame the gods for their troubles.

> Oh, for shame, how the mortals put the blame upon us
> gods, for they say evils come from us, but it is they, rather
> who by their own recklessness win sorrow beyond what is
>   given.
>
> (*Od.* 1.32–34)

The gods may meddle, tempt, deceive, even act badly out of jealousy for human happiness—Penelope hints that the gods did the latter in the case of her marriage. Nevertheless, the stubborn human being with a stout heart and steadfast mind can endure. He or she must be *empedos*, literally "grounded." Penelope and Odysseus share this quality, and it constitutes their true *homophrosune* (like-mindedness). The word *empedos* is used for the bonds that hold Odysseus against the mast to prevent him from being seduced by the Siren's song (12.161) and for the footing that he manages to maintain as he dangles over Charybdis, the whirlpool. In book 19, the Cretan describes Penelope as being like a king whose fame (*kleos*) goes to wide heaven because his land flourishes under good rule and his flocks bear young without fail [*empeda*] (19.107–14). This comparison is made not so much to equate Penelope with a king as to equate a king with a mother whose own firmness secures the family. Whenever she appears in the great hall at Ithaca, Penelope stands against the pillar of the roof. The first time she does this, we may wonder whether she needs the support of the column, but by the end of the Odyssey, we understand that the column, the roof, and the whole house require her support. Finally, the word *empedos* is used at *Odyssey* 23.203 to describe the unshakable bedpost of the marital bed. When Penelope suggests moving the marital bed, Odysseus is upset by the possibility that Penelope has forgotten the fact of its immobility. Like Telemachos earlier, Odysseus momentarily fears that Penelope has forsaken her own essence. But she has not. She has such a firm grip on herself that one wonders whether she would have needed to have been tied to the mast in order to have resisted the Sirens.

Penelope's speech, then, is less an apology for Helen's faults than a modest account of Penelope's own prodigious virtue. Whereas Helen is a goddess of love who acts like a mere woman, Penelope is a mere woman who acts like, or even better than, a god.

CHAPTER SIX

The Poem of Mind

"The true hero," Simone Weil writes in a brief, brilliant, and famous essay, "the true subject matter, the center of the *Iliad* is force" (2003, 57). Force transforms a living being into a corpse and a free individual into a slave. Its principal setting is the battlefield, where warriors cut down other warriors with cold steel and are cut down themselves in turn. At the same time as it annihilates the victim, force intoxicates, overwhelms, brutalizes, and eventually destroys the mighty. Yet Weil, looking through the lens of the Christian Gospels, may have seen the *Iliad* a little too narrowly. She writes as though Homer's poem is an unrelenting indictment of force, and she argues that we "rediscover epic genius" only when we learn that force is never to be admired (69). The Greeks, of course, celebrated the other aspect of force as well, the aspect that is useful and necessary and whose mastery is a virtue. The Iliadic hero earns his lasting fame (*kleos*) through his excellence (*aretē*) in battle. Weil hints at a positive aspect when she admits that the "tempered use of force [is] indispensable to the escape from its machinery" (57). Achilles is partly redeemed from the dehumanizing effect of force by his encounter with Priam. So, it is better to understand the *Iliad* less as a polemic against force than as a serious exploration of force that treats it as one of the great abiding facts of human life and that probes its possibilities, paradoxes, dangers, and limits.

If the true subject of the *Iliad* is force, the true subject of the *Odyssey* is mind. Mind is as germane to the power, mystery, and misery of human life as force and is as worthy of examination. On the plainest level, the

Odyssey answers the *Iliad*. Force is one potent weapon for overcoming the enemy, but mind is the other. Athene points out that battles are won in either of two ways—openly or by stealth. Open, frank, brutal, face-to-face assaults that rely on force are the Iliadic standard. The sword outranks the bow; ambush is demeaning; poison is shameful. In the *Odyssey*, nearly every battle is won by outsmarting the enemy.

Speech is the mind's most powerful instrument for affecting others, and the *Odyssey* is born in an awareness of its power, as both tool and weapon. Speech can reflect and clarify reality. It also possesses the terrible power to falsify reality and to beguile the mind into believing the falsity. The use of speech entails personal responsibility. After the great battle in book 22 of the *Odyssey*, Medon, Phemios, and Leodes—three whose livelihood depended on skill in speech—supplicate Odysseus. Odysseus spares the herald, Medon, who used words artlessly to report the news. He also spares Phemios, the bard, who wove tales that excited innocent pleasure in those that heard. But Leodes receives no mercy. Odysseus reasons that Leodes, as the diviner for the suitors, must have predicted many false things for personal gain. His head "dropped in the dust while he was still speaking," severed from his shoulders by Odysseus's sword (*Od.* 22.329).

The value of the mind is by no means limited to the manipulation of others. Beyond *mētis*, the mind allows a hero both to maintain self-control and to act for the sake of a goal. In the *Iliad*, the goal is lacking. "War expunges every concept of goal, even the goals of war," Weil writes (2003, 59). Everything there tends to dissolve into the exigencies of the moment. The *Odyssey*, in contrast, is consciously structured by goals and becomes meaningless without them. Odysseus's central purpose is to reach home, and Penelope's is to ensure that the House of Odysseus reaches the next generation. The true like-mindedness (*homophrosune*) of husband and wife lies in their commitment to the importance of the *oikos*. Odysseus explains to Nausicaa:

> For nothing is better than this, more steadfast
> than when two people, a man and his wife, keep a harmonious
> household; a thing that brings much distress to the people who
>   hate them
> and pleasure to their well-wishers, and for them the best
>   reputation.
>
>   (*Od.* 6.182–85)

Unfortunately, the importance of the essential orientation to a specific, long-range goal has been undermined by tradition. Roman authors essentially taught that Penelope is more or less as preoccupied with her chastity as is Achilles with his pride. As for Odysseus, we have come to think that he cares for nothing more than the adventure itself. Dante assumed that Odysseus was no family man, and both Tennyson and Kazantzakis made moving literature of the idea. Odysseus is the hero who thirsts for knowledge as much as Achilles thirsts for glory. This is the Ulysses that Tennyson never expected to remain at home.

> . . . And this gray spirit yearning in desire
> To follow knowledge like a sinking star
> Beyond the utmost bound of human thought.
>
> (*Ulysses*, 30–31)

But as provocative as these traditional views of Penelope and Odysseus have been, neither is rooted in Homer. There is plenty of evidence that getting home is foremost in Odysseus's mind. He is the hero who contemplates suicide when his first chance at home is thwarted, who braves the realm of the dead for a second chance, and who rejects an offer of immortality in order to preserve a third opportunity. He is the father who balked at the expedition to Troy (it took Agamemnon a while to convince him) and who is appalled to find that Athene has sent his son on an adventure away from Ithaca.

Another related power of the mind is self-control. This, too, the Iliadic hero lacks. "Nothing in the human matter around him," writes Weil, "puts an interval for reflection between impulse and action" (Weil 2003, 53). All of the *Iliad*'s heroes are like the *Odyssey*'s suitors or Odysseus's crew, who are as impulsive and foolish as children. Like Oscar Wilde, the one thing that they cannot resist is temptation.

When Athene first greets Odysseus on the Ithacan shore, she is tickled by how much she and Odysseus are alike in their penchant for *mētis*.

> You wretch, so devious, never weary of tricks, then you would not
> even in your own country give over your ways of deceiving

and your thievish tales. They are near to you in your very
  nature.
But come, let us talk no more of this for you and I both know
sharp practice, since you are far the best of all mortal
men for counsel and stories, and I among all the divinities
am famous for wit and sharpness.

(Od. 13.293–99)

Nevertheless, the main reason for her admiration and support is another power of his mind.

Always you are the same, and such is the mind within you,
and so I cannot abandon you when you are unhappy,
because you are fluent, and reason closely, and keep your head
  always.
Anyone else come home from wandering would have run
  happily off to see his children and wife in his halls.

(13.330–34)

The phrase "keep your head always" translates the Greek word *echephrōn*, which is used only eight times in the *Odyssey*, here for Odysseus and the other seven times for Penelope.

To have self-control is not, however, to be without emotion. The cold indifference induced by Helen's drug is actually the abandonment of self-control. To their credit, Odysseus and Penelope never deny their deep-felt feelings but also never allow emotion to trump rationality. Odysseus's deep sadness on the shore does not prevent him from casting a skeptical eye on Calypso's offer to help him leave. Strong emotion requires even stronger mental control. In this way too, Penelope and Odysseus are like-minded.

Unfortunately, strength of mind is a more tenuous thing than strength of body. Though Hector cannot easily be transformed into a weakling except by Achilles, those who rely on mental powers must stay alert. Trusting the wrong person can make one an instant fool. If nothing else, gods can certainly get the better of anyone. As Penelope points out, even someone as *epiphrōn* (literally, "on top of the mind") as Eurykleia can be changed into someone who is *aphrōn* (literally, "without a mind").

Dear nurse, the gods have driven you crazy. They are both able
to change a very sensible [*epiphrōn*] person into a senseless
one [*aphrōn*], and to set the light-wit on the way of discretion.

(23.11–13)

Many forces threaten to beguile the mind. In self-delusion, the mind
can become its worst enemy. Penelope is worried about this in her profound reflection on her dilemma in book 19: "So my mind is divided
and starts one way, then another" (19.524). She fears ending up like
Pandareos's daughter, who committed the worst of crimes "when the
madness was upon her" (19.523). The poet explores a variety of threats
to the purpose and mental resolve of Odysseus and his crew in the
adventure books of the *Odyssey* (books 8–12). Every episode offers its
beguilements. Lotus offers narcotic pleasure, and wine undoes Elpenor.
Envy opens the bag of winds; pride provokes Poseidon's curse. Lust invites Circe's magic, and vanity would have crashed everyone at the
Siren's feet if the crew had not been deafened and if Odysseus had not
been bound to the mast.

However much Penelope and Odysseus are alike in their goal and
the strength of their resolve, they differ significantly in how they use
their mental powers. Odysseus is defined by the varied, the multiple, the
diverse. So many of Odysseus's epithets begin with the prefix *polu-*
(many): *Polutropos, poluatlas, poluainos, poluphrōn, polumēchanos*, and,
most important, *polumētis*. Odysseus is multiplicity, seeming never to
be quite the same at any two moments, easily transformed, easily disguised, versatile, slippery, insinuating—the consummate actor. Penelope has no epithets that begin with *polu*. She has little to do with
multiplicity and remains remarkably unified and immovable in her
purpose and strategy. Penelope's spirit is one of concentration. Even
at the one time when Penelope says that she would like to be remembered for her *mētis*, it is a *mētis* qualified by *epiphrōn*: "For how, my
friend, will you learn if I in any way surpass the rest of women,
in mind and thoughtful [*perphrona*] good sense [*mētis*]?" (19.325–26).
As I have already noted, *epiphrōn* is the word Penelope used to char-
acterize the kind of person (e.g., Eurykleia) who is least likely to be
gulled by the gods (23.12).

Both of Penelope's epithets employ the use of compounds built on
the ending *-phrōn*. The noun *phrēn* names the human organ that is the

seat of thought. When Odysseus is given an epithet ending in -*phrōn*, it is *poluphrōn*, in which the prefix *polu-* expresses a multifaceted, polymorphous use of mind that is more like *mētis*.

Can we be more precise about the meaning of *periphrōn*, a word that describes Penelope more than fifty times in the *Odyssey*? Cunliffe's Homeric lexicon (1963) offers the definition "of good sense, wise, sage, prudent"—hardly more than a generic set of words that has been routinely employed by translators for so many Homeric epithets. What does the *peri-* add to the idea of "mind"? The prefix *peri-* can mean "all around, on all sides." For example, the verb *periphuō* means "to grow around; hence, to throw one's arms round a person, embrace someone." Eumaios embraces Telemachos when the latter has returned safely from Sparta; Odysseus embraces his father upon their reunion in the *Odyssey*'s last book. The prefix *peri-* may also mean "going beyond, excelling, surpassing, being superior to." Perhaps it indicates better how Homer means us to understand Penelope in this poem of the mind. Her mind is mind at its best.

"Mindful" might be a good way to render *periphrōn*, especially in the sense that it has been employed in translations of Zen Buddhist texts. It is the power that grasps the meaning of a Zen koan. It is a mental perspicacity that has nothing to do with verbal gymnastics. It is thought that strives to understand, not manipulate; to make clear, not confuse. It is the intellect as Henry David Thoreau described it, which "discerns and rifts its way into the secret of things" (Thoreau 1971, 98).

Once Penelope finds a way for Odysseus to reclaim his true identity, the couple falls into each other's arms without reproval. In a very deft move, Homer shifts the focus decisively from Odysseus to Penelope. The long voyage of suffering that the poetry leads us to believe has been Odysseus's is beautifully transposed onto Penelope.

> And as when the land appears welcome to men who are
> swimming,
> after Poseidon has smashed their strong-built ship on the open
> water,
> pounding it with the weight of wind and the heavy
> seas, and only a few escape the gray water landward
> by swimming, with a thick scurf of salt coated upon them,

and gladly they set foot on the shore, escaping the evil;
so welcome was her husband to her as she looked upon him,
and she could not let him go from the embrace of her white
    arms.

(23.233–40)

The famous simile of the sailor returning home, which Homer initially leads us to think applies to Odysseus, turns out to describe Penelope. We cannot help but feel that hers has been the struggle most arduous, most rigorous, most severe. It would be ideal to end my examination of Penelope on this note, but Homer has more to say.

The abrupt shift of scene to the underworld at the opening of book 24 is the oddest narrative jump in the *Odyssey*. There is no real preparation for it, and we seem, indeed, to be in an entirely different world. For eighty lines, there is not even an allusion to Ithaca or to anything else heretofore significant in the *Odyssey*. The focus is on Troy and its glory. Agamemnon approaches his former comrades in arms Achilles, Patroklos, Antilochos, and Ajax and begins eulogizing Achilles. He recounts the battle for Achilles' corpse, the extreme grief felt by Thetis for her son and by the Achaeans for their champion, the elaborate eighteen-day funeral, the commemorative athletic games, the glorious grave mound erected in Achilles' honor, and the great fame that this most excellent hero is certain to enjoy forever. How much more strongly could it invoke the Iliadic values?

Agamemnon's words make for a pathetic (and somewhat comic) entrance into Hades for the shades of the suitors, those "choice young men" (24.107) of the next generation who will neither get glory nor have any claim to it. They have no heroic virtue, no *aretē*. They are not killed by means that suit heroes, and they complain about their bad luck and the cunning trickery that did them in. As Agamemnon responds to the young men, he credits neither Odysseus nor Odysseus's *mētis* with the victory. Agamemnon's praise is for heroic Penelope.

O fortunate son of Laertes, Odysseus of many devices,
surely you won yourself a wife endowed with great virtue
    [*aretē*].
How good was proved the heart that is in blameless Penelope,
Ikarios' daughter, and how well she remembered Odysseus,

her wedded husband. Thereby the fame [*kleos*] of her virtue
    [*aretē*] shall never
die away, but the immortals will make for the people
of earth a thing of grace in the song for prudent Penelope.

(24.192–98)

The praise could not come from a more unlikely—and thereby credible—source. This is the great misogynist Agamemnon praising a woman; this is the leader of warriors attributing the victory at Ithaca to someone who does not hold a weapon. This is also Homer implicitly comparing Penelope to Achilles. At play here is a reevaluation of the idea of *aretē*, an almost formal transformation that reflects the fundamentally different subjects of the *Iliad* and the *Odyssey*. In the poem of force, the *Iliad*, *aretē* is physical power. In the poem of mind, the *Odyssey*, it is wisdom, whose depth is for Penelope to sound.

Notes

INTRODUCTION

1. Unless otherwise noted, English translations of Homer are by Richmond Lattimore.

2. Three typefaces seem to be the bare minimum for this meticulous scholar, who notes, "In a way I would like to have used a whole range of typefaces, but the restriction to just three does impose some kind of discipline on the editor, and with any luck corresponding limits to the reader's skepticism" (Dawe 1993, 29).

3. In *The Essential Homer* (Homer 2000a), Lombardo omits all of books 2, 3, 7, 14, 15, and 20. He also omits 4.584–839, 8.1–453, 16.321–481, 17.491–606, and 18.107–428.

4. See Horace *Odes* 1.17.19–20; Propertius 2.6.25–28, 2.9.7–8, 3.12.20, 4.5.10.

5. "The Classicist and the Psychopath," foreword to the 1992 reprint of Stanford's 1963 *The Ulysses Theme*. See Boer 1992, viii.

CHAPTER ONE

1. Curiously, Eurynomos is the only named suitor whose death is not accounted for by Homer. A metrical replacement, Eurydamas, otherwise unmentioned in book 22, dies in what seems to be his stead. In two key manuscripts (Marcianus and Caesenas), the name is *Euryalos*, which appears in a list of Trojans cited by Demodokos (*Od.* 8.115). The pattern of the deaths of the fourteen named suitors who die is highly structured. The anomaly of 22.283 is therefore striking. If, indeed, Odysseus kills Eurynomos (not Eurydamas or Euryalos) in this line, the irony of *Odyssey* 2.34 is all the greater.

2. R. D. Dawe finds this passage disturbing. He questions the purpose of announcing an event that took place "at some unspecified time during the last twenty years" (1993, 95). Dawe is surely right that this first evil (or, rather, the acceptance of it) occurred much earlier and is, in this sense, old news. What is new, however, is the public announcement. Without it, most of what follows would be incomprehensible, especially Telemachos's attitude toward the courtship of his mother by the suitors.

3. Telemachos daydreams about his father's return, but even he recognizes this as no more than a daydream, and his journey to the mainland is not motivated by belief in Odysseus's return. I will return to these points in chapter 3, when I investigate Telemachos's character and psychology.

4. We do not know whether the suitors were actively courting Penelope before this. If they were, she was somehow not denying their desires; perhaps she was tolerating their amorous interests.

5. See *Od.* 11.187.

6. Halitherses' prediction is not entirely accurate even from the audience's point of view. We know that Odysseus is in fact not "already somewhere nearby" [που ἤδη ἐγγὺς ἐών] (*Od.* 2.164–65). Nor is he "working out the death and destruction of all these men" (2.165–66).

7. Devereux writes of Telemachos, "Like Hamlet, he is incapable of punishing the suitors, because he unconsciously identifies himself with them" (1957, 381).

8. Do the suitors feel shame about their real intentions? I find the best evidence that they do in the report that Amphimedon makes to the shades in Hades: "At that time [i.e., as soon as Penelope had finished the shroud under duress] an evil spirit, coming from somewhere, brought back Odysseus to the remote part of his estate, where his swineherd was living" (*Od.* 24.149–50). Amphimedon ignores the interval of time between the completion of the shroud and the arrival of Odysseus. This is the time of the suitors' shameful waste of Telemachos's estate. Though he does not totally avoid responsibility for his actions as a suitor, he may be (understandably) eager to minimize them. Why should he make himself seem worse to his fellow shades than he has to? Page calls this passage "among the most perplexing of all mysteries in the *Odyssey*" (1955, 120).

9. Dawe discounts the lines of the *Odyssey*, taking as the original the *Iliad*, "where Agamemnon may reasonably be said to be feeling sorrow" and "where flashing eyes belong more to the outraged field marshal than to the *primus inter pares* domestic villain Antinoös" (1993, 203). Such criticism seems to flow from the commonplace discounting of the domestic situation at Ithaca. Is the purpose of the supposed interpolation meant to unfairly (melodramatically) augment the stature of Antinoös, making him as noble as Agamemnon? One could quibble about the nobility of Agamemnon or to what degree he is held in honor by Homer. More important, the lines do not heighten (or even lower) the moral status of Agamemnon; they are primarily used in the *Iliad* to intensify a sense of danger and threatening power.

10. Contrary to Longinus, I find that the construction of the conflict in the *Odyssey* bears a family resemblance to that of the *Iliad*. In the broadest strokes, the success of character A (Penelope/Chryseis) forces character B (the suitors/Agamemnon) to exert power over character C (Telemachos/Achilles), whose dilemma fuels the plot. Thus, the *Odyssey*—no less than the *Iliad*—opens at a moment of crisis. This initial crisis reveals the major conflict of the plot, which in the *Odyssey*, as in any satisfying story, establishes an anxiety about the outcome.

CHAPTER TWO

1. τῆς δ' αὐτοῦ λύτο γούνατα καὶ φίλον ἦτορ. At the other occurrences, the line is adapted slightly to context.

2. Both Penelope and Laertes feel their knees and heart give way when they recognize Odysseus for the first time (*Od.* 23.205 and 24.345, respectively). Curiously, Homer applies a similar line to describe how the suitors are entranced by the presence of Penelope (18.212). We ought not to forget the first reaction of Andromache to suspicions that Hector is dead: "Within me my own heart rising beats in my mouth, my limbs under me are frozen. Surely some evil is near for the children of Priam" (*Il.* 22.451–53).

3. The link is forged even tighter by the word ἀμφασίη (speechlessness), which appears in Homer only in these two passages.

4. When Helen appears in book 3 of the *Iliad*, Homer makes no attempt to describe her beauty directly but reveals it through the wonder of the old men who behold her. The idea is that if Helen's beauty can set these men to gasping, it must indeed be potent. In the *Odyssey*, the suitors gaze on Penelope, "and all prayed for the privilege of lying beside her" (1.366).

5. Perhaps it should be called "the House of Arkeisios," since Arkeisios, Telemachos's paternal grandfather, is the oldest named member of the line. Nevertheless, I will stick with the name that is better known.

6. It should also be noted that old age, too, makes a man vulnerable. In Hades, Achilles laments the fact that he cannot be home to aid his father, whom he thinks is doubtlessly encountering trouble keeping what he has. "If only for a little while I could come like that to the house of my father, my force and my invincible hands would terrify such men as use force on him and keep him away from his rightful honors" (*Od.* 11.500–503). Achilles can have no news of any threat to his father's right, but he assumes that the aging man is under attack by his own people ("whether he still keeps his position among the Myrmidon hordes, or whether in Hellas and Phthia they have diminished his estate, because old age constrains his hands and feet," 11.495–97). Hostility is to be expected.

7. The anaphora is ignored in every translation that I have consulted. Variety replaces the power of repetition. The Greek reads:

ὧδε γὰρ ἡμετέρην γενεὴν μούνωσε Κρονίων·
μοῦνον Λαέρτην Ἀρκείσιος υἱὸν ἔτικτε,
μοῦνον δ' αὖτ' Ὀδυσῆα πατὴρ τέκεν· αὐτὰρ Ὀδυσσεὺς
μοῦνον ἔμ' ἐν μεγάροισι τεκὼν λίπεν οὐδ' ἀπόνητο.

Lattimore translates:

For so it is that the son of Kronos made ours a single
line. Arkeisios had only a single son, Laertes,
and Laertes had only one son, Odysseus; Odysseus in turn
left only one son, myself, in the halls, and got no profit of me.

8. Penelope is aware that Odysseus's entire family (γόνος) is at risk. See *Od.* 4.741.

9. Seen in another light, the tenuousness of the connection between the generations is counterbalanced by the strength of the bond. Laertes does nothing but pine for his son. Antikleia says that she died out of grief for her son. This is a close family.

10. There is also the story in the *Cypria* that Odysseus would not plow over his son when he was attempting to evade the draft to Troy.

11. For an amusing sampling of the various views, see also Dawe 1993, 671 and 683 nn. 11–14. Dawe, who himself denies (almost willy-nilly) an absurd number of passages as suspicious or inauthentic, writes, "Now whether these words of Penelope's sit well in their present place in the *Odyssey* we have got is debatable, but the qualitative verdict must be that 250–271, and especially Odysseus's own words of 259–270, is a fragment of Homer at his best" (671).

12. This is Hölscher's translation (1996, 134). The original German is "Wer ihn ernst nimmt, geht ganz wie die Freier auf den Leim. Oder wird ein Held, der in den Krieg zieht, davon reden, daß das etwas lebensgefährlich ist. Der sagt vielmehr 'wisch ab dein Gesicht, eine jede Kugel, die trifft ja nicht.'"

13. In the meantime, a few scholars have accepted the directive. Uvo Hölscher (1967) was one of the first. Agatha Thornton endorsed it in her excellent 1970 book *People and Themes in Homer's "Odyssey,"* which, unfortunately, is out of print. John Finley assumes it to be valid in his influential 1978 *Homer's "Odyssey."*

CHAPTER THREE

1. The comparison to Orestes, though provocative and thematic, is invidious. Orestes had greater motivation and much better odds. (In Homer, Orestes is not confronted with the thornier problem of having to decide whether or not to kill his mother.) It seems highly unlikely that Athene should really want Telemachos to make an attack on the suitors. It is not, after all, among the reasons she gives Zeus for going to Ithaca. Ostensibly, she urges Telemachos to go away to find news of his father and then to kill the suitors if he hears that Odysseus is dead. Of course, she knows that Odysseus is not dead. Sending Telemachos away is not a good strategy if his best shot is to attack the suitors off guard. As I have already indicated in chapter 2 of this book, the departure has only served to instigate the threat against Telemachos's life.

2. Athene, too, it turns out, is less than sincere in her exhortation to action. She tries to rally Telemachos by giving him a prophesy that Odysseus is on his way home (*Od.* 1.203–5), but she neglects to add any credible evidence that she knows what she is talking about. She wants to lure Telemachos away from Ithaca, not incite him to fight it out on the spot.

3. The lines (*Od.* 1.356–59) are unflatteringly compared to the near identical lines that Hector uses in the *Iliad* in his farewell to Andromache (6.490–93).

4. The attempt to tie this word to πνέω (root *pnu-*), meaning "breath," has not been successful. Cf. Chantraine 1980, s.v.

5. The epithet describes Medon, Peisenor, an anonymous person (8.586), the Atreidei, Nestor, Menelaos, Amphinomos, Laertes. It is applied to Odysseus twice, but only when the speakers (Alkinoös and Penelope) do not know who they are talking to.

6. Neither thoughtfulness nor wisdom are requisite to the profession of herald, and shrewdness could well do more harm than good, as in Sophocles' *Trachiniae*.

7. Telemachos's statement in line 216 is variously translated as follows: "but it is a wise child who knows his own father" (Butler); "for never yet did any man know his parentage of his own knowledge" (Murray); "I never heard of anyone who knew whose son he was" (Rouse); "it's a wise child that knows its own father" (Rieu); "Who has

known his own engendering?" (Fitzgerald); "who, on his own, has ever known who gave him life?" (Fagels).

8. "Voici un passage dont on a fort abuse contre les femmes, comme si Telemaque avait voulu faire ici une satire contre elles, ce qui est très-faux."

9. "ait voulu douter et faire douter de sa sagesse et de sa fidelité."

10. Schon Porphyrios . . . hat gemeint, daß die Absicht Athenas παίδευσις sei, deshalb schicke sie den Jüngling auf die Reise, und so hat wohl mancher geglaubt, der Dichter wolle uns zeigen, wie Telemachos zum Manne ausreifte. Jetzt traue ich dem Dichter eine solche Tendenz nicht mehr zu. Charakterentwickelung zu verfolgen liegt der hellenischen Poesie, liegt überhaupt den Hellenen fern. Es is auch in den späteren Büchern von einer Veränderung im Wesen Telemachs nichts zu spüren. (Wilamowitz 1927, 106).

11. Allione wrote, "Anzi ci è parso che Telemaco acquistasse consapevolezza della sua maturità con un unico atto di conoscenza" (1963, 24).

12. In the later *Archery at the Dark of the Moon* (1975), Austin finds the epithet πεπνυμένος (*pepnumenos*) to mean "diplomatic": "In the Homeric world, if a young man is noted as gifted with words, a true diplomat, his elders are intimating that here is a man of promise. The ideal young man is one who speaks well but knows when to defer to his elders; this is the man whom the elders will welcome, in due course, into full participation in the community" (77). "*Pepnumenos*," Austin concludes, "is a happy epithet to suggest the Odyssean potential in the boy" (78).

13. However, after his return to Ithaca, Odysseus gives Telemachos explicit instructions on at least two occasions. In book 19, he instructs Telemachos how to go to the palace and pretend that the beggar who is about to show up is no one he knows. He instructs his son to store away whatever weapons are lying about the house ready at hand and "when the suitors miss them and ask you about them, answer and beguile them with soft words [μαλακοῖς ἐπέεσσι παρφάσθαι], (19.5–6) saying . . ."; Odysseus suggests an elaborate lie. Thirty lines later, when Telemachos is amazed at the light cast by Athene (who is helping them to stash the weapons) and wants to talk about it, Odysseus warns him to be more guarded in his emotions: "Hush, and keep it in your mind, and do not ask questions" (19.42). The experience is transformative for Telemachos, who lies awake that night "pondering how, with the help of Athene, he would murder the suitors" (19.51–52). This is the first time he has been confident enough to fully embrace the plan. Still, Telemachos remains without any active effect on the plot until book 21.

14. None of the three statements that Austin pronounces as lying are in fact lies. They are, rather, undisguised statements of what Telemachos believes or has been told by his mother or by Athene. The last statement is perhaps somewhat debatable, because *Odyssey* 1.420 reads: "So spoke Telemachos, but in his heart he knew the immortal goddess" [ὣς φάτο Τηλέμαχος, φρεσὶ δ᾽ ἀθανάτην θεὸν ἔγνω]. There are four good reasons not to think it a lie. First, Athene, whose disguise is not likely to be revealed against her will, has done her best to hide her divinity. Second, Telemachos might have enjoyed a stronger position if the suitors knew that he had divine help. Third, Telemachos, for his part, never again shows such acuity. Fourth, it is even possible that this line is a later interpolation by someone who assumed, as Austin does, that Telemachos ought to know and ought to be cagey about his knowledge. As Stephanie West

points out rightly, the word ἀθανάτην (immortal) "is illogical here, since if Telemachus had not identified his divine visitant as Athena, there would be no reason for him to think specifically of a female divinity" (1988, 125).

15. It is important to reemphasize that the reason Telemachos has not earlier been a threat to the suitors is because he has failed even to comprehend—until shortly before the *Odyssey* opens—that his estate was being pillaged. His naïveté and extreme ineffectuality was one of his chief means of defense. The Telemachy allows Telemachos to perform some activities without thereby becoming any more of an agent in the plot than, say, Nestor or Menelaos.

16. Many authors trace the details of Telemachos's progress. See especially, Delebecque 1958. D'Arms and Hulley maintain, "The development of Telemachus' manhood can be traced in detail, as he gradually gathers confidence, assumes control of many matters in his own home, joins with Odysseus in planning the destruction of the suitors, takes a worthy part in their slaughter when the time comes, and finally stands with Laertes and Odysseus against the numerous relatives of the slain suitors in book XXIV" (1983, 208). P. Jones argues, "But from book 17 onwards, the success of Telemachus' and Odysseus' joint deception is absolutely crucial to their eventual triumph and *it hangs largely on Telemachus' ability to negotiate a continuing deception*" (1988, 505).

17. As soon as the suitors enter the feast, Telemachos reminds them that the house belongs to Odysseus.

So he spoke, and all of them bit their lips in amazement
at Telemachos, and the daring way he had spoken to them.
Now Antinoös, the son of Eupeithes, said to them:
'We Achaians must accept the word of Telemachos,
though it is hard. Now he threatens us very strongly.
Zeus, son of Kronos, stopped us; otherwise we should before now
have put him down in his halls, though he is a lucid speaker.'

(20.268–74)

18. No one seriously thinks that the Cretan is a threat to the suitors' position. He is only a threat to their good name. What if it got out that this decrepit man bested them with the bow? They might become the butt of all sorts of jokes by the Ithacan populace at large. So Penelope retires with very little, if any, sense of relief, since the following day is sure to reveal the groom.

CHAPTER FOUR

1. In book 18, Penelope reminds the suitors of her promise to marry when Telemachos has a beard. She also solicits gifts. This solicitation can only mean that she is announcing her intention to remarry. Otherwise, it would certainly be risky. The gifts are going to restore to Telemachos some of what he has lost recently through the suitors' new strategy.

2. Hermes and Athene continue to maze by bright light.

3. I have slightly altered Lattimore's translation here and wherever necessary in order to render the Greek θέλγω with the English "beguile" consistently throughout the text.

4. Meaning literally, "without trust," the word *apistos* can have two very differ-

ent senses. Once again, a comparison with the Iliad is revealing. In the *Iliad, apistos* always means "not to be trusted, faithless" (*Il.* 3.106, 24.63, 24.207) and is never a compliment. In the *Odyssey*, the word never means that. Instead, *apistos* there means "not believing, incredulous" (*Od.* 14.125, 14.391, 23.72). The vice in the one epic becomes a virtue in the other.

5. Penelope's second and final laugh later in book 18 has been given much attention, According to Daniel Levine, in his article "Penelope's Laugh: *Odyssey* 18.163," scholars have overwhelmingly taken it to be a sign of weakness. "Penelope's laugh has been variously described as pale, idle, inane, useless, helpless, needless, pointless, forced, silly, aimless, improper, artificial, ill-timed, fruitless, feigned, superficial, queer, and foolish" (Levine 1983:172). Levine rejects all such interpretations and sees the laugh as an indication of Penelope's strength. He interprets it as a sign of the *mētis* that she supposedly shares with her husband. I have criticized this approach in the introduction to this book. Levine's view further theorizes that Penelope knows of Odysseus's plan and that she is relishing the idea of its success. In my view, Penelope shows with her laughter in book 18 neither emotional passivity nor cunning superiority. Rather, she demonstrates her intellectual appreciation of the situation. After all, Athene has given Penelope an uncharacteristic and irrational urge to show herself to the suitors. "Eurynome, my heart desires, though before it did not, to show myself to the suitors, although I still hate them." (18.164–65). Indeed, the absurdity of the situation warrants the laughter.

6. The version offered in the scholia may be the oldest but may also be a mere consequence of a misunderstanding of the word for "nightingale" in the text; the later version is from the Attic authors, who felt no great compulsion to retell stories just as they found them. Since the spellings of the two principal names differ from Homer's (*Pandion* for *Pandareos* and *Itys* for *Itylos*), we may, as Joseph Russo points out, be dealing with accounts as different from each other as Sophocles' account of Oedipus is from Homer's (Russo 1992, 100).

7. Russo defends the Procne story by arguing that Penelope implies that the "nightingale killed her own son not by mistake" (1992, 100) when she admits that her own mind is divided between two courses of action. But Penelope is not trying to decide whether to kill her son for revenge.

8. Most translators have tried for neutrality: "in my dream" (Butler); "in a dream though it was" (Murray); "I mean in my dream" (Rouse); "that was in my dream" (Lattimore); "all this in dream" (Fitzgerald).

9. We all know that it is not unusual for one to coolly witness in a dream what would be horrible in real life. Freud would insist that nothing in a dream is what it seems, except the affect, which always is.

10. Dodds notes, "That the common anxiety-dream was as familiar to the author of the *Iliad* as it is to us, we learn from the famous simile: 'as in a dream one flees and another cannot pursue him—the one cannot stir to escape, nor the other to pursue him—so Achilles could not overtake Hector in running, nor Hector escape him' (Iliad, 22.199ff.)" (1951, 106).

11. Apthorp notes: "Helen's drug introduces the danger that he will lose sight of the urgency of his duty to home and family. . . . When the thought crosses Telemachus' mind a little later that his father must be dead (4.292–93) his only reaction is to seek the joyful oblivion of sleep" (1980, 15).

12. Ferrucci argues: "[Proteus] epitomizes the spirit of the whole work. . . . The *Odyssey* is assuredly one of the works in which the problem of identity is most acutely and profoundly perceived. A doubt is often voiced by its characters: And what if I am not what I am? . . . The spirit of Proteus runs through the entire poem" (1980, 34, 37).

13. Scholars have assumed that Proteus is a prophet, though Homer never says so. Lattimore's marginal caption for this section reads, "Capture of the prophetic Old Man of the Sea" (Homer 1965, 76–77), and West cites speculation that the name derives from a connection to prophesy: "His name has been connected with his gift of prophecy, *fatidicus*, cf. πρωτόν, πέπρωται, though the poets audience would probably have derived it from πρῶτος" (1988, 217).

14. The reference to the Elysian fields is a hapax legomenon in Homer and does not appear again in Greek until five hundred years later, in the work of Apollonius Rhodius (4.811), who was consciously mimicking Homer. Although the Elysian fields appear in any encyclopedia of religion as a fact of Greek religion, it is just as likely here that Proteus was putting one over on the gullible Menelaos.

15. The word εὐφραδέως means "in clear or well-chosen terms" (Cunliffe, 1963, s.v.). It is a hapax legomenon in Homer and an extremely rare word in subsequent literature, so this passage defines its use, not the other way around, and cannot tell us much more than we already know.

16. I substitute the translation "artless" for Lattimore's "honorable."

17. Whatever we believe that the early Greeks should have thought about dreams, Penelope's skepticism cannot but ring true to us now. Everyone knows that there are dreams that come to nothing. We may dream of winning a distinction that we know we have little or no chance of enjoying. Many men, says Jocaste in Sophocles's *Oedipus* (981–82), dream of sleeping with their mothers without it ever happening.

18. Sigmund Freud, who reduced all dreams to intrapsychic wish-fulfillment, insisted that antiquity reduced them all to the extrapsychic. He wrote in the *Interpretation of Dreams*, "The pre-scientific view of dreams adopted by the peoples of antiquity was certainly in complete harmony with their view of the universe in general, which led them to project into the external world as though they were realities, things which in fact enjoyed reality only within their own minds" (1965, 38). Even the claim that it was Freud's discovery that no dreams have any other explanation than wish-fulfillment is not quite tenable. Dodds points out that the Hippocratic treatise *On Regimen* "anticipates Freud's principle that the dream is always egocentric" (1951, 119).

19. After all, the major function of dreams, according to Freud, is to allow the dreamer to sleep by disguising the anxiety of thought; and we know that Penelope could use some sleep.

20. Since Penelope is praying to Artemis, she is unlikely to be falsifying her reality or her feeling. A wish for suicide is not shameful in Homer. When reality is overwhelming, one naturally would like escape. Odysseus contemplates suicide (*Od.* 10.51) or wishes to die (10.498). The important thing is that one decides to live, to tough it out.

21. Dawe is perplexed: "If she meant that happy dreams are after all a bad thing, because the waking reality becomes by contrast that much harder to bear, she has notably suppressed the most important part of her thesis" (1993, 730).

22. I adapt Lattimore's translation slightly to emphasize that this is a general philosophy of fame that applies to both men and women. At *Odyssey* 19.325–26 (already

quoted in the text), Penelope has talked about surpassing other women (γυναικῶν ἀλλάων), but she now speaks of human beings of both sexes (ἄνθρωποι and βρότοι). Even so, she clearly has her own case in mind.

23. The word ἀπηνής may mean "ungentle, harsh, rough, hard, insulting, or stubborn," though Cunliffe (1963, s.v.) does not record the last two meanings.

24. From the root σχε- (ἔχω) (Chantraine 1980, 1081).

CHAPTER FIVE

1. "Orderly" is αἴσιμη. The word means "appointed by the will of the god." Specifically what do the gods appoint in this word? "Justice" is the general answer. More accurately, it is balance, moderation, fairness, equality. Eumaios uses the word when he apportions a meal equally to all alike. Mentor and Athene use it to describe Odysseus's moderate and evenhanded style of ruling. Antinoös uses it in the negative to describe someone who overdoes it with wine and loses control.

2. Just as lightly, Eumaios rejected a similar oath sworn to him by the Cretan (14.171).

3. "Baffle" is Lattimore's translation of the problematic word εἴρυσθαι, which might be more modestly rendered by "discover," "spy," or even "know."

4. In the *Iliad*, however, Paris warrants the prefix attached to his name (3.39, 8.769).

5. The method of reasoning characteristic of the analytic school is troubling at its core. If a passage does not conform to what is expected of the writing as formula, analysts judge it an interpolation. But is it not much more likely that any interpolator would follow as closely as possible the formulas and the other obvious characteristics of the master text? I find it more surprising that some scribe has not inserted a few appreciative words by Penelope under the assumption that it would make the poem more Homeric.

6. The word ἄγαμαι could mean "be jealous" or "bear a grudge," which sounds like Ovid's Penelope. Cunliffe cites this passage as an example of the meaning "to be offended or hurt." Hanna Roisman attributes just such a motivation to Penelope. She is supposed to be acting out of the anger that arose from her hurt pride: "For it must have been rather insulting that Odysseus chose to confide in his son rather than his wife" (Roisman, 62).

7. Herodotus 3.154; trans. Grene.

8. The second-person singular has caused trouble. Is Penelope tacitly admitting that she is convinced or that she is on her way to being convinced? Is it a slip of the tongue, as Roisman thinks (Roisman, 65)?

9. Many critics have simplified and trivialized the test of the bed. Heubeck believes that Penelope has all but given in. What the purpose of the test could be for those who believe that Penelope has already recognized Odysseus through his disguise is beyond comprehension. Forcing Penelope to play the coquette is no service to her agency. Winkler attempts to have it both ways: Penelope, he thinks, is only 99 percent sure that this man is Odysseus (1990, 160). The stakes are so high that she must be 100 percent sure. Yet she is sure enough, according to Winkler, to help this man gain sovereign control in the οἶκος. A 1 percent error would give an interloper 100 percent of the household.

Bibliography

Adkins, A. W. H. 1960. *Merit and Responsibility: A Study in Greek Values*. Oxford.
———. 1972. Truth, Κόσμος, and Ἀρετή in the Homeric Poems. CQ 22:5–18.
Allen, W., Jr. 1939. The Theme of the Suitors in the *Odyssey*. TAPA 70:104–24.
Allione, Lydia. 1963. *Telemaco e Penelope nell' Odissea*. Turin: G. Giallichelli.
Amory, Anne. 1966. The Gates of Horn and Ivory. YCS 20:1–58.
Apthorp, M. J. 1980. The Obstacles to Telemachus' Return. CQ 30:1–22.
Armstrong, Richard. 2000. Penelope's Challenge to Her . . . Translators. *Classical and Modern Literature* 20, no. 1:37–76.
Atchity, K. J., and E. J. W. Barber. 1987. Greek Princes and Aegean Princesses: The Role of Women in the Homeric Poems. In *Critical Essays on Homer*, ed. K. Atchity, R. Hogart, and D. Price, 15–36. Boston: G. K. Hall.
Athanassakis, A. N. 1994. The Eagle of Penelope's Dream. AncW 25, no. 1:121–34.
Auffarth, C. von. 1991. *Der drohende Untergang: "Schöpfung" in Mythos und Ritual im alten Orient und in Griechenlend am Beispeil der Odyssee und des Ezechielbuches*. Berlin: Walter de Gruyter.
Austin, N. 1969. Telemachos Polymechanos. *California Studies in Classical Antiquity* (CSCA) 2:45–63.
———. 1975. *Archery at the Dark of the Moon: Poetic Problems in Homer's "Odyssey."* Berkeley: University of California Press.
Bal, Mieke. 1983. The Narrating and the Focalizing: A Theory of the Agents in Narrative. Trans. Jane E. Lewin. *Style* 17:234–69.
Bassett, S. E. 1910. The Suitors of Penelope. TAPA 49:41–52.
Belmont, D. E. 1967. Telemachus and Nausicaa: A Study of Youth. CJ 63:1–9.
Bergren, A. 1981. Helen's "Good Drug": *Odyssey* IV 1–305. In *Contemporary Literary Hermeneutics and Interpretation of Classical Texts*, ed. S. Kresic, 201–14. Ottawa: Ottawa University Press.
Beye, Charles Rowan. 1974. Male and Female in the Homeric Poems. *Ramus* 3:87–101.
Bill, C. J. 1932. Περίφρων Πηνελόπεια. CJ 28:207–9.

Boer, Charles. 1992. The Classicist and the Psychopath. In *The Ulysses Theme: A Study of the Adaptability of a Traditional Hero*, by W. B. Stanford. iii–xix. Dallas: Spring Publications.

Brooks, Peter. 1992. *Reading for the Plot: Design and Intention in Narrative*. Cambridge: Harvard University Press.

Büchner, W. 1940. Die Penelopeszenen in der *Odyssee*. *Hermes*, 75:129–67.

Buitron-Oliver, D., and B. Cohen. 1995. "Between Skylla and Penelope: Female Characters of the *Odyssey* in Archaic and Classical Greek Art." In *The Distaff Side: Representing the Female in Homer's "Odyssey*," ed. B. Cohen, 29–58. Oxford: Oxford University Press.

Butler, Samuel. [1908] 1967. *The Authoress of the "Odyssey."* Reprint, Chicago: University of Chicago Press.

Byre, C. 1988. Penelope and the Suitors before Odysseus: *Odyssey* 18.158–303. *AJP* 109:159–73.

Cave, Terence. 1988. *Recognitions: A Study in Poetics*. Oxford: Oxford University Press.

Chantraine, P. 1980. *Dictionnaire étymologique de la langue grecque*. Paris: Klincksieck.

Clarke, H. W. 1967. *The Art of the "Odyssey."* Englewood Cliffs, N.J.: Prentice-Hall.

———. 1969. Telemachus. In *Homer's "Odyssey": A Critical Handbook*, ed. Conny Nelson, 28–41. Belmont, Calif.: Wadsworth.

Clay, J. S. 1983. *The Wrath of Athena: Gods and Men in the "Odyssey."* Princeton: Princeton University Press.

Cohen, B. 1995. *The Distaff Side: Representing the Female in Homer's "Odyssey."* Oxford: Oxford University Press.

Colakis, M. 1985. The Laughter of the Suitors. *CW* 79:137–41.

Combellack, Frederic. 1983. Wise Penelope and the Contest of the Bow. In *Twentieth-Century Interpretations of the "Odyssey*," ed. H. W. Clarke, 103–11. Englewood Cliffs, N.J.: Prentice-Hall.

Crooke, M. 1898. The Wooing of Penelope. *Folklore*, 121–33.

Cunliffe, Richard John. 1963. *A Lexicon of the Homeric Dialect*. Norman: University of Oklahoma Press.

D'Arms, E. F., and Karl K. Hulley. 1946. "The Oresteia-Story in the *Odyssey*." *TAPA* 77:207–13.

Dawe, R. D. 1993. *The "Odyssey": Translation and Analysis*. Sussex, England: Book Guild.

Delebecque, E. 1958. *Télémaque et la structure de l'Odyssée*. Annales de la Faculté des Lettres d'Aix-en-Provence 21, Editions Ophrys.

———. 1980. *Construction de l'Odyssée*. Paris: Belles Lettres.

Detienne, M., and Jean-Pierre Vernant. 1978. *Cunning Intelligence in Greek Culture and Society*. Trans. Janet Lloyd. Atlantic Highlands, N.J.: Humanities Press.

Devereux, G. 1957. Penelope's Character. *Psychoanalytic Quarterly* 26:378–86.

———. 1976. *Dreams in Greek Tragedy: An Ethno-Psycho-Analytic Study*. Berkeley: University of California Press.

Devereux, G., and D. Kouretas. 1958. Ὁ χαρακτήρ τῆς Πηνελόπης. *Platon* 10:250–55.

Dietz, G. 1971. Das Bett des Odysseus. *Symbolon* 7:9–32.

Dimock, G. E. 1989. *The Unity of the "Odyssey."* Amherst: University of Massachusetts Press.

Dodds, E. R. 1951. *The Greeks and the Irrational*. Berkeley: University of California Press.

Doherty, L. E. 1991. Athena and Penelope as Foils for Odysseus in the *Odyssey*. *Quaderni Urbinati di Cultura Classica* 39:31–44.

———. 1995. *Siren Sings: Gender, Audiences, and Narrators in the "Odyssey."* Ann Arbor: University of Michigan Press.

Eckert, Charles, W. 1963. Initiatory Motifs in the Story of Telemachus. *CJ* 59, no. 2:49–57.

Emlyn-Jones, C. 1984. The Reunion of Penelope and Odysseus. *Greece and Rome.* 33:1–18.

———. 1986. True and Lying Tales in the *Odyssey*. *Greece and Rome.* 33:1–10.

Felson-Rubin, N. 1994. *Regarding Penelope: From Character to Poetics.* Princeton: Princeton University Press.

———. 1996. Penelope's Perspective: Character from Plot. *Reading the "Odyssey": Selected Interpretive Essays,* ed. Seth L. Schein, 163–83. Princeton: Princeton University Press.

Fenik, Bernard C. 1974. *Studies in the "Odyssey."* Hermes Einzelschrift 30. Wiesbaden: F. Steiner.

———. 1978. *Homer: Tradition and Invention.* Leiden: Brill.

Ferrucci, Franco. 1980. *The Poetics of Disguise: The Autobiography of the Work in Homer, Dante, and Shakespeare.* Trans. A. Dunnigan. Ithaca: Cornell University Press.

Finley, John A. 1978. *Homer's "Odyssey."* Cambridge: Harvard University Press.

Finley, M. I. 1955. Marriage, Sale, and Gift in the Homeric World. *Revue Internationale des Droits de l'Antiquité,* 3rd ser., 2:167–94.

———. 1965. *The World of Odysseus.* Rev. ed. New York: Viking.

Foley, H. 1978. "Reverse Similes" and Sex Roles in the *Odyssey*. *Arethusa* 11:7–26.

———. 1995. Penelope as Moral Agent. In *The Distaff Side: Representing the Female in Homer's "Odyssey,"* ed. B. Cohen, Penelope. 93–115. Oxford: Oxford University Press.

Frame, D. 1978. *The Myth of Return in Early Greek Epic.* New Haven: Yale University Press.

Fredricksmeyer, Hardy C. 1997. Penelope Polutropos: The Crux at *Odyssey* 23.218–24. *AJP* 118:487–97.

Freud, Sigmund. [1900] 1965. Trans. James Strachey. *The Interpretation of Dreams.* New York: Basic Books.

Gaskin, R. 1990. Do Homeric Heroes Make Real Decisions? *CQ* 40:1–15.

Gregory, Elizabeth. 1996. Unravelling Penelope: The Construction of the Faithful Wife in Homer's Heroines. *Helios* 23, no. 1:3–20.

Haft, Adele, J. 1984. Odysseus, Idomeneus, and Meriones: The Cretan Lies of *Odyssey* 13–19. *CJ* 79:289–306.

Halverson, John. 1986. The Succession Issue in the *Odyssey*. *Greece and Rome* 33:119–28.

Harrison, A. R. W. 1968. *The Law of Athens.* Vol. 1, *The Family and Property.* Oxford: Clarendon Press.

Harsh, Philip Whaley. 1950. Penelope and Odysseus in *Odyssey* XIX. *AJP* 71:1–21.

Heatherington, M. E. Chaos, Order, and Cunning in the *Odyssey*. *Studies in Philology* 73:225–38.

Heilbrun, Carolyn. 1990. What Was Penelope Unweaving? In *Hamlet's Mother and Other Women.* New York: Ballantine Books.

Helleman, Wendy. 1995a. Homer's Penelope: A Tale of Feminine Arete. *Echos du Monde Classique* 39 n.s. 14: 227–50.

———. 1995b. Penelope as Lady Philosophy. *Phoenix* 49:283–302.

Herodotus. 1987. *The History*. Trans. David Grene. Chicago: University of Chicago Press.

Herzfeld, Michael. 1985a. Gender Pragmatics: Agency, Speech, and Bride-Theft in a Cretan Mountain Village. *Anthropology* 9:25–44.

———. 1985b. *The Poetics of Manhood: Contest and Identity in a Cretan Mountain Village*. Princeton: Princeton University Press.

———. 1986. Within and Without: The Category of "Female" in the Ethnography of Modern Greece. In *Gender and Power in Rural Greece*, ed. Jill Dubisch, 215–33. Princeton: Princeton University Press.

Heubeck, A., Stephanie West, and J. B. Hainsworth. 1988. *A Commentary on Homer's "Odyssey."* Volume 1: Introduction and Books I–VIII. Oxford University Press.

Heubeck, Alfred, and Arie Hoekstra. 1989. *A Commentary on Homer's "Odyssey."* Volume 1: Books IX–XVI. Oxford University Press.

Hexter, Ralph. 1993. *A Guide to the "Odyssey."* New York: Vintage Books.

Hoffer, Stanley E. 1995. Telemachus' Laugh (*Odyssey* 21.105): Deceit, Authority, and Communication in the Bow Contest. *AJP* 116:515–31.

Hogan, James C. 1973. Aristotle's Criticism of Homer in the *Poetics*. *CP* 58:81–108.

Holmberg, Ingrid E. 1997. The Sign of Metis. *Arethusa* 30:1–34.

Hölscher, Uvo. 1978. The Transformation from Folk-Tale to Epic. In *Homer: Tradition and Invention*, ed. Bernard C. Fenik. 51–67. Leiden: Brill.

———. 1989. *Die Odyssee: Epos zwischen Märchen und Roman*. Munich: Beck.

———. 1996. Penelope and the Suitors. In *Reading the "Odyssey": Selected Interpretive Essays*, ed. Seth L. Schein, 133–40. Princeton: Princeton University Press.

Homer. 1731. *L'Odyssée d'Homere*. Trans. Madame [Anne] Dacier. Amsterdam: Chez les Wetsteins & Smith.

———. 1932. *The "Odyssey" of Homer*. Trans. T. E. Lawrence. New York: Oxford University Press.

———. 1937. *The "Odyssey."* Trans. W. H. D. Rouse. New York: New American Library.

———. 1945. *The "Odyssey."* Trans. E. V. Rieu. New York: Penguin.

———. 1963. *The "Odyssey."* Trans. Robert Fitzgerald. Garden City, N.Y.: Doubleday.

———. 1965. Trans. Richmond Lattimore. *The "Odyssey" of Homer*. Chicago: University of Chicago Press.

———. 1969a. *The "Odyssey."* Trans. Herbert Bates. New York: McGraw-Hill.

———. 1969b. *The "Odyssey."* Trans. Samuel Butler. New York: Simon and Schuster.

———. 1995. *The "Odyssey."* 2 vols. Ed. and trans. A. T. Murray. Cambridge: Harvard University Press.

———. 1996. *The "Odyssey."* Trans. Robert Fagels. New York: Viking.

———. 2000a. *The Essential Homer: Selections from the "Iliad" and "Odyssey."* Ed. and trans. Stanley Lombardo. Indianapolis: Hackett.

———. 2000b. *Odyssey*. Trans. Stanley Lombardo. Indianapolis: Hackett.

Hornblower, S. and A. Spawforth. 1996. *The Oxford Classical Dictionary*. Oxford: New York, Oxford University Press.

Jamison, Stephanie. 1999. Penelope and the Pigs: Indic Perspectives on the *Odyssey*. *Classical Antiquity* 18:227–72.

Johnston, S. I. 1994. Penelope and the Erinyes: *Odyssey* 20.61–82. *Helios* 21:137–59.

Jones, P. 1988. The ΚΛΕΟΣ of Telemachus: *Odyssey* 1.95. *AJP* 109:496–506.

Jong, Irene J. F. de. 1985. Eurycleia and Odysseus' Scar. *CQ* 35:517–18.

———. 1987. *Narrators and Focalizers: The Presentation of the Story in the "Iliad."* Amsterdam: Gruner.

———. 2001. *A Narratological Commentary on the "Odyssey."* Cambridge University Press.

Kahn, L. 1980. Ulysse, ou la ruse et la mort. *Critique* 36:116–34.

Kakdridis, J. 1971. The Recognition of Odysseus. In *Homer Revisited*, 151–63. Publications of the New Society of Letters at Lund 64. Lund: Gleerup.

Katz, Marilyn Arthur. 1987. *Penelope's Renown: Meaning and Indeterminacy in Homer's "Odyssey."* Princeton: Princeton University Press.

Kearns, E. 1982. The Return of Odysseus: A Homeric Theoxeny. *CQ* 32:2–8.

Kirk, G. S. 1962. *The Songs of Homer*. Cambridge: Cambridge University Press.

Kurtz, J. G. 1989. The Mind and Heart of Penelope. *New England Classical Newsletter and Journal* 17:11–25.

Lacey, W. K. 1966. Homeric ΗΕΔΝΑ and Penelope's ΚΨΡΙΟΣ. *Journal of Hellenic Studies* 86:55–68.

Lateiner, Donald. 1995. *Sardonic Smile: Nonverbal Behavior in Homeric Epic*. Ann Arbor: University of Michigan Press.

Levine, D. B. 1982. Homeric Laughter and the Unsmiling Suitors. *CJ* 78:97–104.

———. 1983. Penelope's Laugh: *Odyssey* 18.163. *AJP* 104:172–78.

———. 1987. *Flens Matrona et Meretrices Gaudentes:* Penelope and Her Maids. *CW* 81:23–27.

Longinus. 1985. *On the Sublime*. Trans. James A. Arieti and John M. Crossett. New York: E. Mellen Press.

Louden, Bruce. 1999. *The "Odyssey": Structure, Narration, and Meaning*. Baltimore: Johns Hopkins University Press.

Mackail, J. W. 1925. Penelope in the *Odyssey*. *Classical Studies*, 54–75.

Mactoux, M.-M. 1975. *Pénélope: Légende et mythe*. Annales Littéraires de l'Université de Besançon 175. Paris: Belles Lettres.

Malkin, Irad. 1998. *The Returns of Odysseus: Colonization and Ethnicity*. Berkeley: University of California Press.

Marquardt, Patricia. 1985. Penelope Polutropos. *AJP* 106:32–48.

Méautis, G. 1960. Pénélope hésitante. *Paideia* 15:81–86.

Merkelbach, R. 1969. *Undersuchungen zur Odyssee*. Rev. ed. Zetemata: Monographien zur Klassischen Altertumswissenschaft 2. Munich: C. H. Beck.

Merry, W. W. [1878] 1964. *"Odyssey," Books XIII–XXIV*. Reprint, Oxford: Clarendon Press.

Messer, W. S. 1918. *The Dream in Homer and Greek Tragedy*. New York: Columbia University Press.

Morris, J. F. 1983. "Dream Scenes" in Homer: A Study in Variation. *TAPA* 113:39–54.

Morrison, James V. 1992. *Homeric Misdirection: False Predictions in the "Iliad."* Ann Arbor: University of Michigan Press.

Mossé, C. 1981. La femme dans la société homérique. *Klio* 63:149–57.

Murnaghan, S. 1987a. *Disguise and Recognition in the "Odyssey."* Princeton: Princeton University Press.

———. 1987b. Penelope's *agnoia*: Knowledge, Power, and Gender in the *Odyssey*. *Helios* 13:103–13.

———. 1995. The Plan of Athena. In *The Distaff Side: Representing the Female in Homer's "Odyssey,"* ed. B. Cohen, 61–79. Oxford: Oxford University Press.

Nagler, Michael. 1993. Penelope's Male Hand: Gender and Violence in the *Odyssey*. *Colby Quarterly* 29:241–57.

Nagy, Gregory. 1979. *The Best of the Achaeans: Concepts of the Hero in Archaic Greek Poetry*. Baltimore: Johns Hopkins University Press.

———. 1992. Homeric Questions. *TAPA* 122:17–60.

Nortwick, T. van. 1979. Penelope and Nausicaa. *TAPA* 109:269–76.

———. 1983. Penelope as Double Agent: *Odyssey* 21.1–60. *CW* 77:24–25.

Olson, S. D. 1989. The Stories of Helen and Menelaus (*Odyssey* 4.240–89) and the Return of Odysseus. *AJP* 110:387–94.

———. 1990. The Stories of Agamemnon in Homer's *Odyssey*. *TAPA* 120:57–71.

———. 1994. Telemachos' Laugh (*Od*. 21.101–105). *CJ* 89:369–72.

Ovid, and Peter E. Knox. 1995. *Heroides: Selected Epistles*. Cambridge Greek and Latin classics. Cambridge, England and New York: Cambridge University Press.

Page, D. 1955. *The Homeric "Odyssey."* Oxford: Clarendon Press.

———. 1973. *Folktales in Homer's "Odyssey."* Cambridge: Harvard University Press.

Papadopoulou-Belmehdi, Ioanna. 1994. *Le chant de Pénélope*. Paris: Belin.

Peradotto, J. 1990. *Man in the Middle Voice: Name and Narration in the "Odyssey."* Princeton: Princeton University Press.

———. 2002. Prophecy and Persons: Reading Character in the *Odyssey*. *Arethusa* 35:3–15.

Plass, P. 1969. Menelaus and Proteus. *CJ* 65:104.

Podlecki, A. J. 1967. Omens in the *Odyssey*. *Greece and Rome*, 2nd ser., 14:12–23.

Pratt, Louise. 1993. *Lying and Poetry from Homer to Pindar: Falsehood and Deception in Archaic Greek Poetics*. Ann Arbor: University of Michigan Press.

———. 1994. *Odyssey* 19.535–50: On the Interpretation of Dreams and Signs in Homer. *CP* 89:147–52.

Pucci, P. 1982. The Proem of the *Odyssey*. *Arethusa* 15:39–62.

———. 1986. Les figures de la métis dans l'Odyssée. *Metis: Revue d'anthropologie du monde grec ancien*. 1:7–28.

———. 1987. *Odysseus Polutropos: Intertextual Readings in the "Odyssey" and the "Iliad."* Ithaca: Cornell University Press.

———. 1996. The Song of the Sirens. In *Reading the Odyssey: Selected Interpretive Essays*, ed. Seth L. Schein, 191–200. Princeton: Princeton University Press.

Rankin, A. V. 1962. Penelope's Dreams in Books XIX and XX of the *Odyssey*. *Helikon* 2:617–24.

Richardson, N. J. 1983. Recognition Scenes in the *Odyssey* and Ancient Literary Criticism. *Papers of the Liverpool Latin Seminar* 4:219–35.

———. 1990. *The Homeric Narrator*. Nashville, Tenn.: Vanderbilt University Press.

Roisman, H. M. 1987. Penelope's Indignation. *TAPA* 117:59–68.

———. 1994. Like Father Like Son: Telemachus' κέρδεα. *Rheinisches Museum für Philologie* 137, no. 1:1–22.

Rose, Gilbert. 1967. The Quest of Telemachus. *TAPA* 98:391–98.

Russo, J. 1982. Interview and Aftermath: Dream, Fantasy, and Intuition in *Odyssey* 19 and 20. *AJP* 103:4–18.

Russo, J., Manuel Fernandez-Galiano, and Alfred Heubeck. 1992. *Commentary on Homer's Odyssey. Volume II: Books XVII–XXIV*. Oxford University Press.

Russo, J., and B. Simon. 1968. Homeric Psychology and the Oral Epic. *Journal of the History of Ideas* 29:489.

Rutherford, R. B., ed. 1992. *"Odyssey" Books XIX and XX*. Cambridge: Cambridge University Press.

Saïd, S. 1998. *Homère et l'Odyssée*. Paris: Belin.

Schein, S. L. 1995. Female Representations and Interpreting the *Odyssey*. In *The Distaff Side: Representing the Female in Homer's "Odyssey,"* ed. B. Cohen, 17–27. Oxford: Oxford University Press.

Schmiel, R. 1972. Telemachus in Sparta. *TAPA* 103:463–72.

Scodel, R. 1998. The Removal of the Arms, the Recognition with Laertes, and Narrative Tension in the *Odyssey*. *CP* 93:1–17.

Scott, John A. 1917. The Journey Made by Telemachus and Its Influence on the Action of the *Odyssey*. *CJ* 13:420–28.

———. 1936. The First Book of the *Odyssey*. *TAPA* 67:1–6.

———. 1965. *The Unity of Homer*. New York: Biblo and Tannen.

Segal, C. 1983. *Kleos* and Its Ironies in the *Odyssey*. *L'Antiquité Classique* 52:2–47.

Slatkin, L. M. 1996. Composition by Theme and the *Metis* of the *Odyssey*. In *Reading the "Odyssey": Selected Interpretive Essays*, ed. Seth L. Schein, 223–37. Princeton: Princeton University Press.

Stanford, W. B. 1950. Homer's Use of Πολυ- Compounds. *CP* 45:108–10.

———. 1963. *The Ulysses Theme*. Oxford: Blackwell.

Tennyson, Alfred. [1842]. 1970. Ulysses. In *The Norton Anthology of Poetry*, ed. Arthur M. Eastman, et al. New York: Norton.

Thalmann, W. G. 1992. *The "Odyssey": An Epic of Return*. New York: Twayne.

Thiel, H. van. 1991. *Homeri Odyssea*. New York: Georg Olms Verrlag.

Thornton, Agathe. 1970. *People and Themes in Homer's "Odyssey."* London: Methuen.

Thompson, W. E. 1972. Athenian Marriage Pattern: Remarriage. *University of California Studies in Classical Antiquity* 5:211–25.

Thomson, J. A. K. 1914. *Studies in the "Odyssey."* Oxford: Clarendon Press.

Thoreau, Henry David. 1971. *Walden*. Ed. Lyndon Shanley. Princeton: Princeton University Press.

Vernant, J.-P. 1996. The Refusal of Odysseus. In *Reading the Odyssey: Selected Interpretive Essays*, ed. Seth L. Schein, 185–89. Princeton: Princeton University Press.

Walcot, P. [1930] 1970. *Greek Peasants Ancient and Modern: A Comparison of Social and Moral Values*. Reprint, New York: Barnes and Noble.

———. 1977. Odysseus and the Art of Lying. *Ancient Society* 8:1–19.

Wehrli, F. 1959. Penelope und Telemachus. *Museum Helveticum* 16:228–37.

Weil, Simone. 2003. *Simone Weil's "The 'Iliad' or the Poem of Force": A Critical Edition*. Ed. and trans. James P. Holoka. New York: Peter Lange.

West, S. 1981. An Alternative *Nostos* for Odysseus. *Liverpool Classical Monthly* 6:169–75.

———. 1988. Books I–IV. In *A Commentary on Homer's "Odyssey,"* vol. 1, *Introduction and Books I–VIII,* by A. Heubeck, S. West, and J. B. Hainsworth, 49–245. Oxford: Clarendon Press.

Whallon, W. 1960. The Name of Penelope. *GRBS* 3:57–64.

Wilamowitz-Moellendorff, U. von. 1927. *Die Heimkehr des Odysseus.* Berlin: Weidmann.

Winkler, John. 1990. *The Constraints of Desire.* New York: Routledge.

Woodhouse, W. J. 1930. *The Composition of Homer's "Odyssey."* Oxford: Clarendon Press.

Zeitlin, F. I. 1995. Figuring Fidelity in Homer's *Odyssey.* In *The Distaff Side: Representing the Female in Homer's "Odyssey,"* ed. B. Cohen, 117–52. Oxford: Oxford University Press.

———. 1996. *Playing the Other.* Chicago: University of Chicago Press.

Index